INGRID BERGMAN

The Pictorial Treasury of Film Stars

INGRID BERGMAN

by

Curtis F. Brown

General Editor: **TED SENNETT**

GALAHAD BOOKS • NEW YORK CITY

This Galahad Books edition is published by
arrangement with Pyramid Communications, Inc.

Copyright © 1973 by Pyramid Communications, Inc.

ISBN 0-88365-164-5

Library of Congress Catalog Card Number 73-90217

Printed in the United States of America

FOR HAYDEN GOLDBERG
ANOTHER ARDENT
INGRID BERGMAN ADMIRER

PREFACE

By TED SENNETT

"The movies!" Flickering lights in the darkness that stirred our imaginations and haunted our dreams. All of us cherish memories of "going to the movies" to gasp at feats of derring-do, to roar with laughter at clownish antics, to weep at acts of noble sacrifice. For many filmgoers, the events on the screen were not only larger than life, but also more mysterious, more fascinating, and—when times were bad—more rewarding. And if audiences could be blamed for preferring movies to life, they never seemed to notice, or care.

Of course the movies have always been more than a source of wish-fulfillment or a repository for nostalgic memories. From the first unsteady images to today's most experimental efforts, motion pictures have mirrored America's social history, and over the decades they have developed into an internationally esteemed art.

As social history, movies reflect our changing tastes, styles, and ideas. To our amusement, they show us how we looked and behaved: flappers with bobbed hair and bee-stung lips cavorting at "wild" parties; gangsters and G-men in striped suits and wide-brimmed hats exchanging gunfire in city streets; pompadoured "swing-shift" Susies and dashing servicemen, "working for Uncle Sam." To our chagrin, they show us the innocent (and sometimes not so innocent) lies we believed: that love triumphs over all adversity and even comes to broad-shouldered lady executives; that war is an heroic and virtually bloodless activity; that fame and success can be achieved indiscriminately by chorus girls, scientists, football players, and artists. To our edification, they show us how we felt about marriage in the twenties, crime in the thirties, war in the forties, big business in the fifties, and youth in the sixties. (Presumably future filmgoers will know how we felt about sex in the seventies.)

As an influential art, motion pictures are being studied and analyzed as never before by young filmgoers who are excited by the medium's past accomplishments and its even greater potential for the future. The rich body of films from *Intolerance* to *The Godfather;* the work of directors from Griffith to Kubrick; the uses of film for documenting events, ideas, and even emotions—these are the abundant materials from which film courses and film societies are being created across the country.

THE PICTORIAL TREASURY OF FILM STARS also draws on these materials, encompassing in a series of publications all the people, the trends, and the concepts that have contributed to motion pictures as nostalgia, as social history, and as art. The books in the series range as widely as the camera-eye can take us, from the distant past when artists with a vision of film's possibilities shaped a new form of expression, to the immediate future, when the medium may well undergo changes as innovative as the first primitive movements.

THE PICTORIAL TREASURY OF FILM STARS is a tribute to achievement: to the charismatic stars who linger in all our memories, and to the gifted people behind the cameras: the directors, the producers, the writers, the editors, the cameramen. It is also a salute to everyone who loves movies, forgives their failures, and acknowledges their shortcomings, who attends Bogart and Marx Brothers revivals and Ingmar Bergman retrospectives and festivals of forthcoming American and European films.

"The movies!" The cameras turn and the flickering images begin. And again we settle back to watch the screen, hoping to see a dream made real, an idea made palpable, or a promise fulfilled. On that unquenchable hope alone, the movies will endure.

ACKNOWLEDGMENTS

For the photographs in this book, thanks are due *Movie Star News* and the collections of Jerry Vermilye and Gene Andrewski. For his advice and encouragement during its writing, special thanks to Ted Sennett.

CONTENTS

INTRODUCTION

Once a star, always a star. True? Not necessarily. How many person-alities, having flickered fitfully on the screen in a few starring parts, survived as stars—if they survived at all? Samuel Goldwyn told the movie public that Anna Sten was a star, and proved himself wrong when he displayed her in Zola's *Nana*, Tolstoy's *Resurrection*, and *The Wedding Night*. If foreign nonentities like Garbo, Dietrich, Colman, and Boyer could be made into American stars, the reasoning went, then others like them—Gwili Andre, Lil Dagover, Tala Birell, and Fernand Gravet, for example—could, too. They were wrong.

But once a superstar, it seems, always a superstar. Garbo, Dietrich, Crawford, Davis, Gable, Tracy—despite many poor roles, some indif-ferent guidance by routine directors, and less than heaven-made costar castings, they have retained their status as superstars. No attempt to explain what constitutes a superstar and, once having been so ordained, what mesmerizing power the superstar must maintain over the public to hold the title, has ever been satisfactory. The most that can be said, perhaps, is that although stars may twinkle for a while, superstars blaze forever.

Ingrid Bergman is among the exalted ranks of superstars. Despite a roller coaster career—careful nurturing into stardom under David O. Selznick's aegis, post-Selznick faltering, an artistically disastrous alli-ance with a gifted Italian film director, and a return to success in mostly weakly directed films—Bergman is still considered a potent

13

screen personality. "There are only seven movie stars in the world whose name alone will induce American bankers to lend money for movie productions," Cary Grant once said, "and the only woman on the list is Ingrid Bergman." An overstatement, admittedly: Katharine Hepburn, Bette Davis, and Joan Crawford continue to make films. But Bergman is assuredly one of those stars.

Throughout her American film career and afterwards, one of Bergman's main problems has been her leading men. Great directors, it appears, are not enough. Under Hitchcock, Grant and Bergman struck imperishable sparks; with Gregory Peck, Joseph Cotten, and Michael Wilding hardly a glimmer. It is, to the movie audience, somehow conceivable that there would be intellectual as well as sexual attraction between Bergman and Humphrey Bogart, Bergman and Gary Cooper, Bergman and Grant. But between her and Anthony Quinn in *The Visit*, or between her and Tony Perkins? There is something that makes these alliances difficult to believe and the evidence is on the screen.

A wide range of roles suggests that Ingrid Bergman is at her best as examples of ideal womanhood. That is not to say that she is at her best in virginal roles. This would mean that her greatest performances were as Sister Benedict in *The Bells of St. Mary's* and as the Maid of Orleans in *Joan of Arc*, which is light-years away from the truth. A fairer statement would be that Bergman embodies the most human, provocative, and cherishable qualities that we ordinarily associate with women at their most womanly—innate strength overcoming a passing vulnerability, and an untarnished beauty that inspires in both men and women a pride in human dignity.

A lonely, orphaned childhood, escape into the fantasy world of the theater, then films, marriage, and motherhood, international acclaim as a star of the first magnitude, then another escape, this time into a headlined love affair with a renowned film director, international scandal and banishment from Hollywood, eight years and a third marriage later, a return to cheering and weeping crowds...

It reads like a film script. It isn't; it's the Bergman story.

Ingrid Bergman was born on August 29, 1915, in Stockholm, Sweden, the only child of Justus Bergman and Friedel Adler, a German from Hamburg who died when Ingrid was two. Her father was a painter and photographer who ran a camera shop on the ground floor of the apartment building where they lived, which was located on the Strandvägen, one of Stockholm's most beautiful streets. According to her own account, Bergman was a shy and withdrawn girl who did not have many young friends. When she was eleven, a year before her father died, he took her to see a Swedish play, *Patrasket*, by Hjalmar Bergman (no relation). The stories and plays she had made up and acted out in the theater of her imagination paled beside seeing real people pretending to be other people.

CHAPTER I

THE EARLY YEARS

Six months after Justus Bergman's death, his spinster sister, who had raised Ingrid, died. Alone once more, Ingrid went to live with her father's brother, who had five children, only one of whom was Ingrid's age. Until she was seventeen, she attended a private school, the famous Stockholm Lyceum for Girls. There she conquered her natural shyness by reading dramatic poems before her classmates and also for guests in her uncle's home.

Although she received little or no encouragement from her relatives in her dramatic ambitions, Ingrid auditioned for the School of the Royal Dramatic Theater in Stockholm. She passed the entrance requirement by acting a portion of Strindberg's *The Dream Play*, a comedy turn in which she portrayed a peasant girl teasing a youth, and an excerpt from Rostand's *L'Aiglon*, one of Bernhardt's greatest vehicles. After only a year of study and performances in leading roles, from 1933 to 1934, she was offered a contract by Sweden's leading movie company, Svenskfilmindustri. One of her classmates at the Royal Dramatic Theater was

At age five, with father.

BRANNINGAR (The Surf) *(1935)*.

Gunnar Björnstrand, who years later gave unforgettable performances in such Ingmar Bergman films as *The Seventh Seal*, *Winter Light*, *Persona*, and many others. Recalling her natural, untheatrical appeal, Björnstrand has said, "She gave the impression of total stability. She has willpower and an unbelievable memory. Learning was a snap for her." Thirty years later, they were to costar in Ingrid Bergman's one-picture return to Swedish films.

During her year at the School of the Royal Dramatic Theater, Bergman met, on a blind date, Peter Aron Lindstrom, ten years older than she, and already a successful, handsome young dentist who was studying to be a physician. Lindstrom's encouragement to accept the film offer, combined with her own ambition, led to her first movie, *Munkbrogreven (The Count of the Monk's Bridge)*, released in 1934. She was nineteen years old and played the minor role of a hotel

17

maid in a contemporary comedy about a band of merrymakers bent on painting the town—in this case, Stockholm—red. Reviewers in the daily papers noted Bergman in her film debut; one critic (in *Folkes Dagblad*) remarked that the actress had "an unusual way of speaking" and another (in *Svenska Dagbladet*) observed that she was "a beautiful and statuesque girl."

The following year, 1935, Bergman appeared in four films. In *Branningar (The Surf)*, a tale of carnality and contrition vaguely reminiscent of *The Scarlet Letter*, she played the female lead, a girl who stoically bears the illegitimate child of an erring minister. The critic of *Dagens Nyheter* praised her credibility in a role requiring tenderness and faithfulness. Her second film that year was *Swedenhielms (The Swedenhielm Family)*, a domestic comedy-drama involving a wealthy girl (Bergman) who is engaged to the impecunious son of a great but scatterbrained

SWEDENHIELMS (1935). With Gosta Ekman and director Gustav Molander.

VALBORGSMASSOAFTON (Walpurgis Night) *(1935). With Lars Hanson.*

scientist. When the picture was shown in New York that September, a month after its Stockholm premiere, *The New York Times* critic saw no reason even to note her performance. However, in Germany the *Berlin am Mittag*, reporting on the movie's showing at the Venice Film Festival, singled out Bergman's performance for its emotional quality. *Swedenhielms* marked her first film

under Gustaf Molander, who was to direct her in several more pictures, most recently in *Stimulantia*, made at the Svenskfilmindustri studio in 1964.

Her fourth picture released in 1935 was *Valborgsmassoafton (Walpurgis Night)*, in which she played opposite Lars Hanson. (Hanson, one of Sweden's most popular romantic idols, had starred with Garbo in *Gösta Berling's*

19

Saga in Sweden, and had gone to Hollywood to appear with her in *The Divine Woman.*) Also in the cast was Victor Sjöstrom (Seastrom), the distinguished Swedish actor-director who had directed Hanson and Lillian Gish in *The Scarlet Letter* and *The Wind*, and, many years later, portrayed the venerable professor in Ingmar Bergman's *Wild Strawberries*.

Valborgsmassoafton cast Ingrid Bergman as a woman in love with a man who is caught in a loveless and childless marriage. When his wife commits suicide—after killing a blackmailer who knew of her abortion to avoid having an unwanted child—Bergman and Hanson are united in a loving and fruitful marriage. Seastrom played Hanson's father, a newspaper editor. The picture was warmly greeted in the national press, and six years later when the film was exhibited in New York (to take advantage of Bergman's Hollywood success) the *New York Daily News* expressed indignation that "such a subject as abortion should ever have found its way into celluloid," though conceding that "the film...has an emotional quality that cannot be gainsaid."

Bergman was again directed by Molander and once more cast opposite Hanson in the first of her two 1936 pictures. *Pa Solsidan (On the Sunny Side)* told the light-weight story of how the jealous stirrings of a husband (Hanson) are safely stilled when his sister marries the man whom he thought was drawn to his wife (Bergman). Despite the slight plot—thin to the point of translucency— Swedish critics took Bergman to their collective heart, pronouncing her a performer who was "blindingly beautiful," who acted "with strong inspiration," who had "matured as an actress and as a woman. One simply must give up before her beauty and talent." One paper, *Nya Daglit Allehander*, paid her the ultimate accolade when it said that Bergman "not only supported [Hanson] superbly; she sometimes was his absolute equal." In a characteristically less exalted tone, *Variety*, upon the film's New York release a few months later, allowed that *Pa Solsidan* "should prove a best seller in the 'Svensk nabes'," adding that its female star should "rate a Hollywood berth." *The New York Times* was delighted by "the natural charm of Ingrid Bergman, the young Stockholm actress whose star has risen so rapidly in the Scandinavian film firmament."

Intermezzo, Bergman's other 1936 film, was to take her to that Hollywood berth three years later. Again sensitively directed by Molander, in a screenplay he coauthored from his original story,

INTERMEZZO (1936).
With Gosta Ekman.

DOLLAR (1938). With Georg Rydeberg.

lent acting" (*Aftonbladet*), but also singled out as a motion picture that "does honor both to Svenskfilmindustri and the Swedish film in general" (*Svenska Dagbladet*). That Bergman's importation into America was imminent and did not necessarily spring full-blown from the Selznick International forces, is suggested by the review that appeared in *Variety*, which asserted that "Ingrid Bergman's star is destined for Hollywood."

Bergman was to make five more pictures before reaching Hollywood. In 1937, no Bergman films were released. On July 10, she married Peter Lindstrom, who had continued his studies to become a medical doctor. At twenty-two, Bergman was an experienced film actress with five pictures to her credit.

In 1938, Bergman appeared in three films, two of them under the continuing guidance of Molander. The first, *Dollar*, was a bedroom farce by Hjalmar Bergman, in which the beautiful actress played a beautiful actress (as she was to do again many years later in *Indiscreet*). It was her first glossy high comedy of mores and morals among the well-to-do, and Bergman, according to *Svenska Dagbladet*, outshone the other members of the cast "partly because of her dominant role, far removed from the ones she usually plays." The

Bergman portrayed a gifted pianist-accompanist who has a passionate love affair with a world-famous violinist who is married and the father of two children. Realizing the futility of their liaison, Bergman leaves him, allowing him to return to his forgiving wife. The Swedish press was even more ecstatic than usual about Bergman. "Ingrid Bergman adds a new victory to her past ones," announced the *Ny Tid*. The movie as a whole was not only praised for its "superb music and the interesting conflict" and "excel-

22

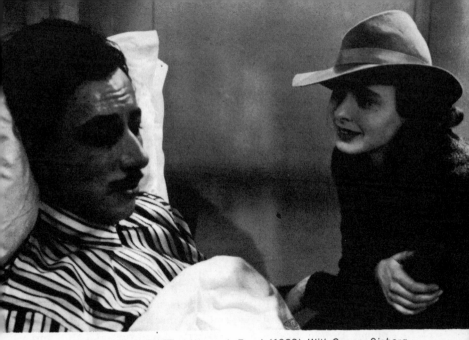

EN KVINNAS ANSIKTE (A Woman's Face) *(1938). With Gunnar Sjoberg.*

review commented also on her "superb comedy timing and lustrous appearance."

The second of the 1938 films was *En Kvinnas Ansikte (A Woman's Face)*. This picture enabled Bergman to depict extremes of both evil and good. A facially disfigured blackmailer, she undergoes successful plastic surgery at the hands of a famous surgeon. Transformed into a beautiful woman and spiritually reborn in the process, she follows, up to the crucial point, her diabolical mentor's command to murder his rich young nephew so that he may inherit a fortune. At the last moment, however, Berg-

man shoots the malevolent schemer instead.

As preposterous as all this sounds, it was remade three years later into one of Joan Crawford's valedictory pictures as an MGM contract star. Under George Cukor's expert direction, Crawford, Melvyn Douglas, and Conrad Veidt turned an improbable script into an irresistibly entertaining movie. (One wonders if Bergman's Swedish version had what must be one of the most fatuous exchanges of dialogue in film history. Veidt asks Crawford if she likes "music—symphonies, concertos?" She replies with Crawford self-

23

assurance, "Some symphonies. Most concertos.")

Both the Swedish and American reviewers were kind to *En Kvinnas Ansikte*, the *Stockholms-Tidningen* calling the film "first class." In 1939, *The New York Times* noted that this "cosmetic tour de force was a surprise, and not altogether an unhappy one either," adding that "the beautiful Ingrid Bergman... has already been discovered by Hollywood and will be seen shortly in Mr. Selznick's *Intermezzo*."

On September 20, 1938, a month before the Swedish release of *En Kvinnas Ansikte*, Friedel Pia Lindstrom was born. At the time, Bergman remarked to the Swedish press, "Why shouldn't an actress have babies? It's perfectly natural."

Die Vier Gesellen (The Four Companions), Bergman's third picture to be released in 1938, was made for UFA in Germany. (Between films, Bergman sometimes visited her mother's relatives in that country. With her gift for languages, she learned to speak and read German.) The plot for this film resembles one that Twentieth Century-Fox used many times in the thirties and forties—an energetic band of bachelor girls pool their talents and resources to make a go of some enterprise or other (in the case of the Bergman film, an advertising agency), and, in the process, land husbands. Among the variations offered in *Die Vier Gesellen:* one girl commits a sexual indiscretion that forces her to marry her boy friend, another girl abandons the agency for a career as a fine artist. Bergman played the business partner who holds out longest against marriage, but finally succumbs. Among the supporting cast was sixty-five-year-old Leo Slezak, the great German operatic tenor and the father of actor Walter Slezak. In the case of this routine film, even the Swedish reviewers seemed unable to summon up much enthusiasm for their favorite daughter: "Chatty and lacking interest" *(Aftonbladet)*. "Too long-winded and thin to generate any real interest" *(Svenska Dagbladet)*. The *Social-Demokraten* found Bergman "self-assured, elegant, and fresh as a daisy," but unexpectedly handed the acting honors to Ursula Herking, "a dark, ugly girl," as the aspiring painter.

In 1939, Gustav Molander directed Bergman again in a sophisticated comedy entitled *En Enda Natt (Only One Night)*. Here, Bergman, as a wealthy society girl, was called upon to resist the advances of a circus employee, who is the illegitimate son of her guardian. In the end, the ardent young man returns to carnival life and his mistress. His father's plan to refine his son by throwing him at

DIE VIER GESELLEN (The Four Companions) *(1938). With Hans Sohnker.*

his ward (Bergman) has not worked. Although today, the plot sounds innocent enough, by thirties' standards it was fairly outspoken, dealing as it did with illegitimacy and extramarital sex. A foreshadowing of the kind of role at which Bergman was to become adept can be seen in the review of the film that appeared in the *Social-Demokraten:* "Bergman, playing the upper-class girl, represents a rare kind of woman with erotic complexes. Miss Bergman handles the role with great finesse." In her Hollywood career, the actress appeared several times as an outwardly proper-appearing girl (or matron) within whom, however, smoldered the fires of pas-

sion—*Intermezzo: A Love Story, Casablanca, Indiscreet,* and *The Yellow Rolls-Royce,* for example.

Bergman's last picture before departing for the United States was *Juninatten (A June Night).* By the time of its release in Sweden, in 1940, Bergman had already been signed by Selznick to star in his remake of *Intermezzo,* her 1936 success. Again, in *Juninatten* Bergman was cast as a wronged woman. Hoping to terminate an affair, she narrowly misses death when her lover, intending to kill himself, accidentally shoots her. After the man's trial, during which Bergman explains the true circumstances, thereby lightening the man's sentence, she is forced to leave town.

EN ENDA NATT (Only One Night)
(1939). *With Edvin Adolphson.*

JUNINATTEN (A June Night) *(1940)*.

All ends happily when Bergman, now in Stockholm, finds the right man to marry. (Appearing also in the picture was Alf Kjellin, whose performance in *Torment* (1944), a highly charged drama written by Ingmar Bergman, sent him to Hollywood.)

If it were not for the fact that Bergman almost invariably received glowing reviews for her performances, one would suspect that the accolades that greeted *Juninatten* were intended as a "bon voyage" farewell to Sweden's favorite female star, who by the time of the film's release had arrived in Hollywood to take up a new phase in her career.

In scanning Bergman's Swedish film career, it is obvious that the actress had the ability and force of personality to make many of her films seem better than they actually were. Her winning beauty and confidence in all her roles somehow spilled over to the rest of the film and made it appear to be more of a triumph than it was. Bergman's recognized talent to lend credibility to whatever role she played— and in some of her Hollywood films she was oddly, if not wrongly, cast —finds its roots in the broad scope of parts she was called upon to play in her Swedish "apprenticeship," from girls innocent in the ways of the world to women very much experienced in them.

With New York movie critics — at least those who had seen some of the imports at the "Svensk nabes" — raving about the luminous beauty and unmistakable acting talent of a Swedish actress named Ingrid Bergman, it was clear that somebody in Hollywood would woo her and win her to a contract. Fortunately, a venturesome, independent producer decided to introduce Bergman to America.

In the summmer of 1938, when David O. Selznick was already well along with his plans to film *Gone With the Wind*, Elsa Neuberger, his New York-based assistant story editor and talent scout, alerted him to a young featured actress she had seen in a Swedish film called *Intermezzo*. With his personally supervised productions of *The Prisoner of Zenda* and *Nothing Sacred* among 1937's top box-office successes, and *The Adventures of Tom Sawyer* launched a few months earlier that year, the prestigious producer had let his staff know that he was interested in acquiring new star material for his producing company, Selznick International.

Selznick saw *Intermezzo* for himself and was taken as much with the romantic story as with what he called "the combination of exciting beauty and fresh purity" of its leading lady. He dispatched Kay Brown, his chief story editor in New York, to go to Stockholm and

CHAPTER II

HOLLYWOOD STAR

persuade Miss Bergman — or, as it turned out, Mrs. Peter Lindstrom, a dentist's wife and mother of a baby girl — to come to Hollywood and star in an English-language version of *Intermezzo*.

At first, Bergman was reluctant to leave her family — her husband's intensive medical studies would not allow him to go, and Pia was still too young to make such a long trip. In the end, however, Selznick's offer of a one-picture agreement, rather than the usual seven-year contract, convinced her. If she was a success, her family would then be able to join her in a year's time. Bergman agreed, and arrived in Hollywood, alone, in the spring of 1939, ready for work.

At the outset of his association with Bergman, Selznick had second thoughts about casting her in the *Intermezzo* remake. Despite his admiration for her Nordic beauty and warm, sensitive screen personality, he wavered, and at first thought of casting Loretta Young and Charles Boyer, among others, in the remake. But having decided on Leslie Howard, who at the time was portraying Ashley Wilkes in *Gone With the Wind*,

28

INTERMEZZO: A LOVE STORY (1939). With Cecil Kellaway and Leslie Howard.

Selznick pressed ahead with his plans for *Intermezzo* as Bergman's American film debut. At one point he thought of changing her name to Ingrid Lindstrom, but decided it was not sufficiently memorable. Besides, Bergman wanted to retain her professional name—she had invested five years in making it known throughout Sweden.

With her natural flair for languages, Bergman learned English quickly under the experienced tutelage of Ruth Roberts, an MGM language coach who had recently drilled Hedy Lamarr. Bergman's proficiency improved as filming on *Intermezzo* continued.

By now, Selznick had decided to call the picture *Intermezzo: A Love Story*, to obviate any confusion in the public's mind as to what an "intermezzo" might be. Yet this was 1939, and though the romance between the married violinist and the pianist was idyllic, it had to be made clear that the woman portrayed by Bergman was basically bad, however tender her feelings toward the man she loved. The audience must be reminded that adultery has unhappy consequences. John Halliday, cast as Leslie Howard's confidant, says pointedly to Bergman at the picture's turning point, when she renounces her lover: "You've taken something recklessly. You must pay for it. It will cost you more than you reckon." Bergman replies simply: "I'm ready."

As filming progressed during the summer of 1939, Selznick was increasingly impressed and delighted with Bergman's evident limitless capacity for hard work and long hours, and her wholehearted commitment to making the picture a success.

When the movie was released in October, 1939, it was a resounding success. *The New York Times* reported: "There is that incandescence about Miss Bergman, that spiritual spark which makes us believe that Selznick has found another great lady of the screen." When the picture opened in London three months later (as *Escape to Happiness*), novelist Graham Greene wrote in his review for *The Spectator:* "The film is most worth seeing for the new star, Miss Ingrid Bergman, who is as natural as her name. What star before has made her first appearance on the international screen with a highlight gleaming on her nose tip? That gleam is typical of a performance that doesn't give the effect of acting at all, but of living—without make-up."

Leslie Howard, the established star of the film as well as its associate producer, and Edna Best as the wronged wife, seemed studied and a little stagey beside the more spontaneous young actress.

It would have been surprising

30

had it turned out otherwise. Selznick had cannily arranged for the entire film to be an almost literal duplicate of the original Swedish success. In fact, those who saw both the Swedish and the American versions at the time, must have rubbed their eyes. The director, Gregory Ratoff (replacing William Wyler), was under specific instructions from Selznick to copy, virtually shot for shot, Molander's *Intermezzo*. Even the soulful theme music from the original

INTERMEZZO: A LOVE STORY (1939). With Leslie Howard.

INTERMEZZO: A LOVE STORY (1939). With Edna Best.

Intermezzo was retained—wisely, as it developed, for the haunting melody that Heinz Provost had composed for violin and orchestra (strongly reminiscent of a leitmotiv in Wagner's *Tristan und Isolde*), with English words added by Robert Henning, became a national favorite. Even Bergman's playing of Christian Sinding's *Rustle of Spring* inspired a revival of that semiclassical piano work in homes throughout America.

With a major star launched beyond his most optimistic hopes, Selznick presented his "discovery" with a seven-year contract. But Selznick, an unusually literate and imaginative man by any standards, was stumped for a likely vehicle for his star. The cultivated producer who had brought scrupulously faithful adaptations of *David Copperfield*, *Anna Karenina*, *A Tale of Two Cities*, and *Rebecca* to the screen might have provided his new star with a film version of Ibsen's *A Doll's House* perhaps, or less likely, *Hedda Gabler*. Bergman herself persuaded Selznick at least to consider filming the story of Joan of Arc, a role she had long nourished an ambition to play. However, since the British were

America's allies during World War II and thus a faithful historical treatment of the saint's life would involve showing the English in an unflattering light, the idea, at least as far as Selznick International was concerned, had to be dropped.

A radiant personality and an accomplished actress had taken America by storm. But nothing happened for Bergman—on film—for two years. That Selznick was unable to create a prestigious production for his new long-term contract star not only shaped Bergman's Hollywood career for the next several years, as a Selznick loan-out property, but at least partly accounts for her impulsive break with the Hollywood system soon after she became free of her Selznick contract.

When Bergman returned to America, in January of 1940, from a five-month vacation in Sweden with her family, she returned with Pia, now nearly a year and a half old. Peter Lindstrom, now a medical doctor and professor at the Swedish Royal Academy of Medicine, was again unable to accompany his wife since he was of military age and living on a continent at war.

There being no need for her in Hollywood, Bergman remained in New York, growing increasingly restive because Selznick had no plans for her. Then, Broadway producer Vinton Freedley, who was planning a revival of *Liliom*, Ferenc Molnar's celebrated play, sent Bergman the script. He hoped she would consent to play the female lead, Julie, a Viennese girl in love with a callous carnival barker. With Selznick's permission (at least, he reasoned, her name would be before the public), Bergman accepted the offer. Burgess Meredith played the title role, and their friendship during the three months the play was scheduled to run, from March through May of 1940, is one of Bergman's pleasantest memories. "He would call me 'You big Swede,'" she later recalled, "and I laughed and loved it."

The critics were delighted with Bergman's American stage debut: "It is nice to have Miss Bergman about," Burns Mantle wrote in the *New York Daily News*. "She is honest, sensitive and carefully schooled." In his *New York Times* review, Brooks Atkinson expressed his enthusiasm: "Miss Bergman keeps the part wholly alive and lightens it from within with luminous beauty."

In September of that year, Selznick, against his better judgment, yielded to Bergman's pleas to let her appear in another film before she got stale and the public forgot her. On profitable (to Selznick's company) loan-out terms with Columbia Pictures, he arranged for his Swedish star to begin work on *Adam Had Four Sons*. Routine in every way, it was nevertheless the first picture Bergman had made in over a year. Gregory Ratoff was again her director.

Adam Had Four Sons turned out to be a disappointment, offset only by the fact of Bergman's return to the screen and by a characteristically salt-and-peppery performance by Helen Westley. Set in the first quarter of this century, it centers on Emilie Gallatin (Bergman), a French governess who is employed by an American family composed of Adam Stoddard (Warner Baxter), his ailing wife, Molly (Fay Wray), and their sons Jack (Richard Denning), David (Johnny Downs), Chris (Robert Shaw), and Phillip (Charles Lind). After Mrs. Stoddard's death, financial troubles beset the family and Emilie, who has become a beloved household fixture, is reluctantly dismissed.

Years later, when the boys have grown to manhood and the Stoddards are prosperous again with the help of wise old Cousin Philippa (Westley), Emilie is restored to their midst as housekeeper. David Stoddard, meanwhile, has married Hester (Susan Hayward), a malicious flirt who, by seducing one of her brothers-in-law, nearly ruins her marriage. However, Emilie, who would rather be thought wicked than have Adam learn the truth, makes it appear that she was the temptress. Later, Hester overplays her hand, and is brought down when she is exposed as the real cause of domestic discord. Emilie is finally raised to a state of married bliss when Adam, who up to now has not evinced any real romantic interest in her, asks, "Won't you share my legacy with me?"

Although Bergman manages to sail serenely through the heavy weather of this teacup tempest, it is hardly a picture worthy of either her talent, her reputation, or her status as a Selznick star. Rather, it represents a regression to the most vapid of her lesser Swedish films. When *Adam Had Four Sons* opened in March 1941, *The New York Times* granted Bergman's "restrained and understanding performance," but aptly termed the picture an "antique tear-jerker."

Bergman's naturally strong personal presence contrasts awkwardly with Baxter's tepid acting in an equally lukewarm role. If the viewer chooses to let his attention stray from the dreary spectacle of Bergman's decade-long romantic thrall to Baxter, he can amuse himself with such unlikely lines as the one Hayward purrs to Bergman soon after they meet: "What does a woman think of when she crosses the ocean to be the governess to

ADAM HAD FOUR SONS (1941). With Richard Denning, Johnny Downs, Helen Westley, Warner Baxter, Susan Hayward.

ADAM HAD FOUR SONS (1941). With Warner Baxter.

RAGE IN HEAVEN (1941). With Robert Montgomery and George Sanders.

RAGE IN HEAVEN (1941). With George Sanders.

four grown men?"

In November 1940, a few days after completing her role in this picture, Bergman was loaned to MGM to appear in a film version of James Hilton's 1932 novel, *Rage in Heaven*. The prospects seemed bright. Translations to the screen of the British writer's *Lost Horizon* and *Goodbye, Mr. Chips* had been acclaimed by the critics and the public. The words "based on the novel by James Hilton" had considerable appeal for millions of readers of current fiction. (Not so in the case of the still underrated *We Are Not Alone*, a gloomy but moving Warner Brothers film of 1940, in which Paul Muni gave what many consider his most sensitive performance.)

Rage in Heaven, however, was not a popular success. Bergman's costar, Robert Montgomery, it was rumored, was being "punished" by MGM, who cast him in this medium-budget, "throwaway" picture. (Montgomery had publicly uttered unflattering home truths about the movie industry.) W. S. Van Dyke II, assigned to direct *Rage in Heaven*, was well known for his speed in getting a story onto film in much less time, and for far less money, than more painstaking directors. Although *Rage in Heaven* was by no means sloppily made, it had a distinct low-budget appearance, despite Van Dyke's

lavishing nearly eight weeks on it. On the credit side, in addition to its two attractive "names," the film departed from the merely routine by offering George Sanders as the hero and Lucile Watson in her customary role as a suave, Junoesque matron.

Set in contemporary England, *Rage in Heaven* deals with the disintegration of a paranoiac, Philip Monrell (Montgomery), heir to an industrial fortune and escapee from a French mental institution where, unknown to his mother (Watson), he has undergone treatment. Returning to England, he courts and marries Stella Bergen (Bergman), his mother's secretary-companion. Feeling inferior to his stable, attractive friend, Ward Andrews (Sanders), Philip attempts to manage the family business. His ineptness in industrial matters causes unrest among the employees, but after Ward's competency averts a factory riot, Philip tries, unsuccessfully but undetected, to murder him. Meanwhile, Philip has grown insanely suspicious of Stella, imagining that she and Ward are having a love affair. Seeking to destroy their imagined liaison by making it appear that Ward killed him, Philip fatally stabs himself. After Ward is convicted of the "crime," Stella visits Dr. Rameau (Oscar Homolka), a French psychiatrist who had treated Philip, and gains the evidence she needs to exonerate Ward.

As melodramatic as the movie is, it has an effective brooding atmosphere reminiscent of some of Bergman's best Swedish pictures —*Valborgsmassoafton*, *En Kvinnas Ansikte*, and *Juninatten*. Additionally, Montgomery and Bergman make an interesting combination. His steely coolness in suggesting barely contained madness complements her convincing portrayal of a loving, but blindly loyal wife. Sanders, dropping his amusing, supercilious mannerisms, turns in a forthright and manly performance.

But again, the film was clearly a time-marker for Bergman until Selznick could find her a property to allow her talent full range, unconfined by a film in which she was called upon to do little else than lend credence to barely credible situations. Surprisingly, the usually skillful and trenchant dialogue of British novelist Christopher Isherwood, who collaborated on the screenplay with Robert Thoeren, is nowhere evident in *Rage in Heaven*. The movie's only claim to literacy, in fact, is the source of its questionably relevant title, poet William Blake: "A Robin Redbreast in a cage/ Puts all heaven in a rage."

When *Rage in Heaven* opened in New York in March 1941, one week before *Adam Had Four Sons*, the *Herald Tribune* deplored the conspicuous waste of Ingrid Bergman: "If our screen keeps overlooking her great talent much longer, it will be a really black mark against it."

"In my first three movies in Hollywood, I played the same kind of woman," Bergman has said, recalling her uphill fight to play the floozy in *Dr. Jekyll and Mr. Hyde*. "I felt I must change. I wanted something I could get my teeth into."

She got it. In December of 1940, after completion of *Rage in Heaven* and a week's rest, Bergman found that her next loan-out assignment was to be as Spencer Tracy's pure fiancée in the MGM big-budget remake of Robert Louis Stevenson's classic. Bergman resisted the typecasting. "I want to play the prostitute," she told Selznick, Tracy, and director Victor Fleming. Lana Turner, an MGM contract player being groomed for stardom, took the studio's "advice" and exchanged roles with Bergman.

Bergman's firm insistence proved a turning point in her career. Had she played the innocuous heroine, she doubtless would have done it splendidly. But by demanding and getting the role of the guttersnipe barmaid originally intended for Turner, she gave the bravura performance that had been

DR. JEKYLL AND MR. HYDE (1941). With Spencer Tracy.

expected from Tracy, and it brought her sleeping career to vibrant life.

It is difficult to say for certain, but one infers that it was Bergman's, not Selznick's fight—and victory. Indications are that it was a combination of her stubborness and Tracy's sympathy for her situation that turned the tide in Bergman's favor. It was Tracy, she says, who insisted that she be granted a screen test for the role of Ivy Peterson. After the test, she recalls,

Tracy said to Fleming, "Vic, you don't have to develop the film. She's our Ivy, and you've got to give it to her."

Fleming filmed *Dr. Jekyll and Mr. Hyde* at considerable peril. Rouben Mamoulian's version, ten years earlier, had earned Fredric March an Academy Award as Best Actor. Its technical effects were astonishing (they still are) and, except for March's too-simian makeup in the later stages of Hyde's transformations, it was a

39

DR. JEKYLL AND MR. HYDE (1941). As the barmaid, Ivy Peterson.

film that would be hard to surpass. But Fleming, who had just directed *Gone With the Wind*, wanted to do the film and he wanted Tracy in the dual role. The actor knew he was neither psychologically nor physically right for a handsome, dapper man-about-London who becomes a terrifying monster. But he yielded, humanly, to flattery from studio executives that a major star like him could do no wrong. They were mistaken.

In London of the 1880s, Dr. Henry Jekyll (Tracy) believes that there are distinct good and evil powers in all men. Elaborating on his idea, he outrages Sir Charles Emery (Donald Crisp), father of his fiancée, Beatrix (Turner). That evening, in pursuit of corroboration of his theory, Dr. Jekyll encounters a barmaid and prostitute, Ivy Peterson (Bergman), and escorts her to her mean lodging. Assuming he is a customer for her favors, she attempts, unsuccessfully, to seduce the good doctor. Later, in the laboratory adjoining his house, Dr. Jekyll drinks an elixir that liberates an uninhibited and malevolent alterego. As Mr. Hyde, he returns repeatedly to Ivy, inflicting increasing cruelty upon her. When Ivy consults kindly Dr. Jekyll as to how to rid herself of Mr. Hyde, she does not foresee that, as Hyde, Jekyll will remember and resent these visits. Angry, Hyde becomes ever more violent towards her, finally murdering her. No longer able to control the Hyde manifestation, Jekyll, in the presence of Sir Charles, involuntarily changes into Hyde and kills Sir Charles to keep the secret inviolate. Struggling with pursuing police, he is overcome and killed. In death, he reverts, to everyone's horror, to his "real" identity as Dr. Jekyll.

The studio and director Victor Fleming spared no expense in making the film. The sets are impeccably furnished; Adrian's costumes are beautiful. Unfortunately, the imagination expended on the film was pretentious and John Lee Mahin's screenplay was more absurd than chilling. In the forties Hollywood was beginning to "discover" Freud, and MGM wanted to make its contribution to the trend. Peter Ballbusch designed "montage" sequences to symbolize the ambivalence in Jekyll/Hyde's subconscious struggle between Beatrix Emery, his spotless intended, and Ivy Peterson, the object of Hyde's erotic obsession. In these murky interludes, Beatrix was symbolized as white flowers, while Ivy was made to wallow in a pit of mud. Even Joseph Ruttenberg's ingenious photography was unable to disguise this ponderous approach to popularized Freud.

Bergman's performance was a tour de force and a revelation to viewers who had seen her only in her previous American films. *The New York Times* singled her out as the highlight of the film: "The young Swedish actress proves again that a shining talent can sometimes lift itself above an impossibly written role. ... Of all the actors, only Miss Bergman has emerged with some measure of honor." The actress' scenes of flirtation with Tracy as Jekyll are a remarkable blend of erotic coquettishness and pitiable vulnerability; her climactic scenes with the bestial Hyde are truly terrifying in their projection of fear and panic. Ironically, the film, planned as a vehicle to demonstrate Tracy's unlimited versatility, became instead a personal triumph for Ingrid Bergman.

Her work in *Dr. Jekyll and Mr. Hyde* completed at the end of February 1941, Bergman was once again "between pictures." She had made three films, one after another, in half a year. Now she could join her husband. Since the previous fall, Dr. Lindstrom had been studying neurosurgery at the University of Rochester, New York. Bergman and Pia moved there and the Lindstrom family was reunited for a while.

By the end of a month or so,

DR. JEKYLL AND MR. HYDE (1941).
With Spencer Tracy.

Bergman found the life of a doctor's wife enervating. "It's awful to sit around for months trying to find something to do," she recalled later. "I couldn't understand the reason for these long layoffs. David Selznick was too fussy; nothing was good enough. Either the story wasn't right for me or the part wasn't big enough. I didn't care how short the part was as long as it was a good acting part."

While visiting Kay Brown, Selznick's right-hand executive on the East Coast, in New York City that spring, Bergman kept after Selznick to find her more work. Then it occurred to the producer that in the absence of suitable film roles for the actress, she was a natural for the name part in a stage revival of Eugene O'Neill's *Anna Christie*. At that time, John Houseman, who had cofounded the sensationally successful Mercury Theatre with Orson Welles a few years before, was conducting a season at the Lobero Theatre in Santa Barbara, California, for the development of Selznick performers and scripts. (Selznick's newest discovery, Phyllis Isley Walker, later known as Jennifer Jones, was trying her wings at the Lobero in a new one-act play by William Saroyan, *Hello, Out There*.) Houseman recalls that "Ingrid Bergman was a joy to work with. She was eager, passionate, well prepared, and she gave me everything I asked for except the feeling that Anna was sick and corrupted and destroyed; one had the conviction that beneath her period skirt her underclothes were starched, clean and sweet smelling. It was a success—with a real Hollywood, Selznick-promoted opening."

The revival opened in Santa Barbara in July, 1941, moved the following month to the Curran Theatre in San Francisco, then, redirected by Margaret Webster, played at the Maplewood Theatre, New Jersey, in September. Reviewing the production, *The New York Times* wrote: "Miss Bergman, an excellent actress and a lovely young woman, made an interesting, and at many times a touching, Anna."

Again idle, Bergman continued to badger Selznick to keep her busy. At that time, another of the once popular Hollywood quests— "Who would be the perfect actress for the part of . . .?"—was under way. Paramount was searching for the "perfect" actress to play Maria in their forthcoming screen adaptation of Ernest Hemingway's bestseller, *For Whom the Bell Tolls*, and the public was being kept abreast of developments by an active publicity department. Bergman wanted the role, and Selznick sensed that with cropped hair and her usual minimum of makeup, she

CASABLANCA (1942). With Dooley Wilson and Humphrey Bogart.

would be splendid as the bronzed and windswept, rough-and-ready guerrilla heroine of the novel, which dealt with the recent Spanish Civil War. Selznick began a campaign to persuade Paramount to cast Bergman. "I won't rest until you get the part," he told her.

Paramount, however, was not interested. Everyone agreed that the studio had the ideal Robert Jordan in Gary Cooper, already signed to the role. But Bergman was Swedish and too ladylike, studio powers said—despite her much-

discussed virtuoso performance as the low-born Londoner in *Dr. Jekyll.* At a meeting with Hemingway in San Francisco, arranged by Selznick, the author presented the actress with a copy of his novel inscribed, "For Ingrid Bergman, who is the Maria of this story." Selznick publicized the incident, convinced that it would clinch the deal he wanted. Months passed, and at last Paramount announced that it had cast Vera Zorina, a svelte, coolly elegant, Berlin-born Norwegian ballerina-turned-

CASABLANCA (1942).
With director Michael Curtiz.

The picture begins in 1940, after the fall of France. Refugees from Hitler's Europe flee to Casablanca, where they hope to acquire exit visas to Lisbon and thence to the United States. An expatriate American, Rick Blaine (Bogart), runs an international café where refugees go for news, rumors—anything that will lead to escape from pursuing Nazis. Heinrich Strasser (Conrad Veidt), a hedonistic Nazi major who fancies caviar and champagne, comes to Casablanca seeking the murderer of two German couriers who were carrying two highly prized letters of transit. Ugarte (Peter Lorre), a nervous informer, has the letters and implores Rick to hide them. Ugarte is shot by the police. Cooperating with Strasser is Captain Louis Renault (Claude Rains), Casablanca's opportunistic prefect of police. Also in Casablanca are Victor Laszlo (Paul Henreid), an important Czech Resistance leader, and his wife, Ilsa (Bergman). They need visas to get to America, where Laszlo can continue his anti-Nazi work.

A flashback reveals that just before the Germans occupied Paris, Rick and Ilsa were lovers. They had planned to flee Paris before the Nazis arrived, but Ilsa, for no apparent reason, deserted Rick. When the Laszlos try to obtain visas from the unctuous

actress. Deeply disappointed, Bergman, on the rebound, gratefully accepted an offer from Warner Brothers to costar in a picture with Humphrey Bogart, fast becoming that studio's top male drawing card.

Selznick still insisted that Bergman would play Maria in *For Whom the Bell Tolls* and he predicted that it would at least win her a nomination for an Academy Award.

The film Bergman and Bogart made together transformed them overnight into superstars. The film was *Casablanca*.

CASABLANCA (1942). With Sydney Greenstreet and Paul Henreid.

Señor Ferrari (Sydney Green-street), proprietor of the Blue Parrot Café and leader of Casablanca's black market, he sends them to Rick, whom he suspects of having the letters Ugarte left behind. Ilsa begs Rick for the letters, but embittered by his memory of Paris, he refuses. Desperate but still in love with Rick, Ilsa almost brings herself to kill him for the letters. She explains that she thought she was Laszlo's widow when they had their affair, having assumed her husband died in a concentration camp. When she learned he was alive, she left Rick to return to her husband.

Rick tells Ilsa they will use the letters of transit themselves, and he tricks Renault into thinking he will deliver Laszlo into his hands to be turned over to Strasser if Renault lets Ilsa and him escape from Casablanca. At the airport, Rick reveals to Renault that it is really the Laszlos who are going to leave. Although Ilsa and Rick are still in love, Rick convinces her that Laszlo's work is more important. Strasser, tipped off by Renault, arrives at the airport to stop the Laszlos' flight, but Rick shoots him dead. Moved by Rick's personal sacrifice, Renault does not arrest him.

CASABLANCA (1942). With Claude Rains, Paul Henreid, Humphrey Bogart.

A compelling script by Julius and Philip Epstein and Howard Koch, Michael Curtiz' sleight-of-hand direction that cunningly diverts attention from weaknesses of plot, and above all, the miraculous pairing of co-stars, arguably make *Casablanca* Bergman's best—and certainly most cherished—film. If proof is needed that the Bergman-Bogart combination gave the picture its special character, one has only to consider that Ann Sheridan and Ronald Reagan were originally cast as Ilsa and Rick, and Dennis Morgan as Laszlo, the Czech freedom fighter. Luminously feminine, Nordic Bergman and swarthy, American tough-guy Bogart went far beyond being merely a pair of screen lovers professionally fulfilling front-office hopes for a box-office bonanza. Together, they created two unforgettable individuals whose interaction never fails to fascinate.

For all Bogart's burly brusqueness, he projects persuasively the world-weariness of an intellectual idealist turned sour. Rick smuggled arms to a defeated Ethiopia; like Robert Jordan in *For Whom the Bell Tolls*, he fought in vain against Franco's Spanish fascists, and he fell in love with a woman who deserted him. Little wonder that his ethical code through most of the film's action is, "I stick my neck out for nobody. ... I'm the only cause I'm interested in." He finds spiritual balm in the cynical character played by Rains ("I blow with the wind, and the prevailing wind happens to be Vichy"; "I'm only a poor corrupt official"), and comradeship with his café's piano player, Sam (Dooley Wilson).

Bergman, on the other hand, has the more difficult role, that of a vulnerable woman desperately torn between emotion and duty. Her former lover, Bogart, has changed, choosing to live for the moment and letting those destroy themselves who will; her husband, Henreid, is a passionately dedicated anti-Nazi idealist. That Bergman's ardent portrayal projects believably and humanly the turmoil of being attracted to these opposite temperaments is testimony to her trained skill and great strength as an actress. In no other role has she demonstrated so well her ability to suggest a woman of romantic susceptibility who also has a strong sense of ethical commitment.

The Bergman-Bogart chemistry works because they persuade us that two intelligent sensibilities, drawn to one another in an adult love affair, have become alienated by events they cannot control. The Paris flashback scenes, taking place just before the Nazi invasion, are played against a symbolic musical background ("Perfidia" alternating with "Deutschland über Alles")

idyll-shattering bombardment ("Was that cannon fire, or is it my heart pounding?" Bergman asks Bogart). The rekindling of the old flame, despite themselves, is symbolized by Wilson's reluctant playing again of the hauntingly beautiful song of their Paris days, "As Time Goes By." By the film's end, they deal maturely — and in character — with a situation impossible otherwise to resolve convincingly. (Veidt, of course, could have melodramatically killed a martyred Henreid, leaving the way open for the lovers to fly off together for a conventionally happy — and completely disappointing — ending.)

In a recent television interview, Bergman discussed the difficulty of working with an improvised script during the filming of *Casablanca*. She recalled that the cast frequently would not know what their lines or situations would be from day to day, and that none of them knew how the tangled plot would be resolved until the final scene was shot. Doubtless, the tentative atmosphere contributed to the actors' convincing depiction of the characters' uncertainty as to what is to become of them. (None of these incidental script problems prevented the authors from receiving a joint Academy Award for that year's Best Screenplay.)

Despite *Casablanca's* apocalyptic background of desperate political refugees caught up in a world of intrigue and betrayal, its many unsavory characters, and its cynical observations on the mendacity of human conduct, it comes across as a hymn to the tenacity of the human spirit. Arthur Edeson's superb chiaroscuro lighting and photography, all deep shadows and highlights (except, quite properly, the fully lit Paris love scenes), reflect the dilemma of the character Bergman plays. Her disappearance into the radiant mist at the end of the film leaves behind, on the rain-washed airstrip, a Bogart reborn through their shared sacrifice.

This is how *The New York Times* summed up the essence of *Casablanca*: "The Warners here have a picture which makes the spine tingle and the heart take a leap....The crackling dialogue which has been packed into this film...is of the best....The performances of the actors are all of the first order, but especially those of Mr. Bogart and Miss Bergman....One of the year's most exciting and trenchant films."

It is a pity that Bergman and Bogart never again appeared together. Under Curtiz' Academy Award-winning direction, each one brought to the other qualities that spelled much more than box office.

In the summer of 1942, *Casablanca* and *For Whom the Bell Tolls* had gone into production at approximately the same time. Soon, rumors were rife that, after two weeks of shooting, Vera Zorina was not working out as the Maria of Paramount's dreams. Word spread quickly that the fine, chiseled features of the actress were not enhanced by the short haircut the role required. The studio swallowed its pride and contacted Selznick: Would Bergman be available to play Maria when she finished *Casablanca* at the end of August?

Selznick thought that Bergman was entitled to a two-week rest after finishing her picture at Warners. But Bergman, determined not to let this chance slip by, insisted that she could report to Paramount, ready for work, the day after she finished *Casablanca*. Under Selznick's supervision, she received a short, but becoming, haircut, then sped to the California High Sierras, where location sequences were being shot. The cast, crew, and director, Sam Wood, were awaiting her. For the next two months, until the end of October 1942, filming proceeded confidently on *For Whom the Bell Tolls*.

Set in the era of the Spanish Civil War in 1937, *For Whom the Bell Tolls* follows the fortunes of Robert Jordan (Gary Cooper), a volunteer on the side of the Loyalist ("Republican") resisters to the

FOR WHOM THE BELL TOLLS (1943). As Maria.

51

Fascist ("Nationalist") revolutionaries. Assigned to a band of guerrillas to help them blow up a bridge that will thwart the Falangists' advance near Segovia, Jordan experiences grave doubts about the enterprise, but he decides to go ahead with the plan anyway.

In the band of peasant Spanish fighters are its leader, El Sordo (Joseph Calleia); the weak and drunken former leader, Pablo (Akim Tamiroff); and his dominating woman, Pilar (Katina Paxinou), a source of great fighting strength and earthy humor. Also in the group is Maria (Bergman), a girl whose parents (her father was mayor of their city) were executed as resisters and who was herself a victim of multiple rape.

At first, Jordan struggles against the attraction he feels toward Maria ("You've got to understand, Maria, I'm in this to the finish. I can't have anything serious in my life"), but they fall in love nevertheless. They enjoy a few hours of passion together, after which Jordan leaves the guerrillas to fulfill the mission, a task that he knows will end in his death. He consoles himself with the knowledge that he and Maria have asserted human dignity in their selfless love for one another.

That it seems not at all inappropriate for a twenty-eight-year-old Swedish actress to play a Spanish peasant guerrilla of nineteen attests to the force of Bergman's personality and the public's willing acceptance of her as an artist of considerable versatility. One suspends disbelief, too, when confronted by broad-accented actors—one Russian, the other Greek—as Spaniards, when the talents involved are played with the ripe theatricality of Tamiroff and of Paxinou, who justly won an Oscar as Best Supporting Actress for her delineation of Pilar. However, under Sam Wood's workmanlike but unremarkable direction, Gary Cooper is not at his best. In a role ill-suited to his greatest strength—a gift for wry humor and boyish charm—the actor seems less a doomed anti-Fascist American idealist named Robert Jordan, than a doomed, anti-Fascist American idealist cast as Gary Cooper.

The well-known excisions of the novel aside—its frank, sleeping-bag dialogue and its pointed political orientation—Dudley Nichols' screenplay (novelist Louis Bromfield had written an earlier adaptation) is notably faithful in tone and content to Hemingway's powerful work. However, this fidelity works to both advantage and disadvantage. The reader of the novel readily accepts the elemental simplicity of Hemingway's mock-Spanish speech when it falls on the inner ear. But when spoken aloud—

FOR WHOM THE BELL TOLLS (1943). With Akim Tamiroff, Gary Cooper,
Katina Paxinou, Vladimir Sokoloff, Arturo de Cordova.

FOR WHOM THE BELL TOLLS (1943). With Gary Cooper, Katina Paxinou.

even by skilled actors—it sounds less like authentic Spanish-into-English and more like English that never was. The first exchange of dialogue between Bergman and Cooper is effective: "How are you called?" "Maria. And you?" "Roberto. Been here long?" "Three months. They shaved my head in Valliliod." Here, the lines are sufficiently brief not to distract. To Bergman's credit, it must be noted that the girlish appeal with which she imbues her part carries her successfully through her famous speech to Cooper: "Oh, Roberto, I—I don't know how to kiss or I would kiss you. Where do the noses go? Always I've wondered where the noses would go... I always thought they would be in the way."

On the other hand, not even Cooper, despite his ability to heighten realism by appearing to improvise his lines, could make much of his important speech to Bergman, in which he explains his presence in civil war-torn Spain: "The Nazis and Fascists are just as much against democracy as they are against the Communists, and they're using your country as a proving ground for the war machinery—their tanks and dive bombers and stuff like that." Such painfully jéjune lines do not help *For Whom the Bell Tolls* gain in serious interest over the years. At the same time, Bergman's "nose" speech quoted previously, and trivial details like Tamiroff's "You try to prowoke me, Inglés? I do not prowoke," remain delightfully in the memory.

The nearly three-hour film (it covers less than three days' action) was handsomely photographed in Technicolor, under Ray Rennahan's supervision, in the California High Sierras. The exterior location sequences and the simulated studio "exteriors" are superbly matched, a complicated and painstaking process handled with great skill by production designer William Cameron Menzies. Bergman's first appearance in a color film revealed much of her natural beauty for the first time on the screen. However, dazzling Technicolor lessened the impact that harsh, black-and-white cinematography might have given to the grim realities of Hemingway's story. Drab poverty, Spartan heroism, and dusty death tend to come second to spectacular visual effects.

For Whom the Bell Tolls suffers seriously in the cut version shown on television. The viewer requires the omitted scenes (those including the character André Massart, played by George Coulouris, for example) to understand the film's narrative intention.

In addition to a strong cast, a script that dodges some of Heming-

At the premiere of
FOR WHOM THE BELL TOLLS.

by Victor Young—rousing and, at times, moving and haunting.

Although critic James Agee, writing in *The Nation*, disliked the political bowdlerizing of Hemingway's novel, he declared that "Miss Bergman not only bears a startling resemblance to an imaginable human being; she really knows how to act, in a blend of poetic grace with quiet realism which almost never appears in American pictures....Her confession of the rape is an exquisitely managed tearjerker. Her final scene of farewell is shattering to watch...She seems really to have studied what a young woman might feel and look like in such a situation....It is devastating and wonderful to see." Bosley Crowther of *The New York Times* observed that Bergman and Cooper "are fine, though limited in their opportunities. Miss Bergman is perhaps a shade too gay."

For Whom the Bell Tolls is a picture that gains much of its power to move and disturb from its harshly contrasting themes of the tragic necessity of dying, perhaps futilely, in the cause of freedom, and the fleeting time allotted to us for intense personal emotion: "How much time have we left?" "A lifetime, Maria."

For her performance in the film, Bergman was nominated for an Academy Award as 1943's Best Actress — fulfilling Selznick's

way's chief points but is still sensitive to his style, and scenic splendor of possibly too overwhelming a magnificence, the picture has a richly atmospheric musical score

55

promise. The Oscar winner was Jennifer Jones, for her performance in *The Song of Bernadette.*

During World War II, Bergman, like many other entertainment personalities, toured the United States on behalf of the government's War Bond drives and visited military camps to entertain servicemen. In February 1943, her travels, in company with four-year-old Pia and a maid, took her to Minneapolis and environs to make *Swedes in America,* a two-reel propaganda short depicting the lives of Swedish-Americans in a country at war. Made by the Office of War Information, it was made particularly to be shown in neutral Sweden.

Chronological complications, at least as far as release dates of Bergman's films are concerned, enter at this point. During the war, Hollywood's film production was at an all-time high to satisfy entertainment demands of battle-weary fighting men and of a public hungry for diversion from swing shifts, rationing, and grim headlines. Because of government priorities and restrictions, raw film stock was at a premium. Thus, many studios —Warner Brothers especially— "hoarded" their completed top-budget movies. Not knowing how long the war would continue, they maintained a backlog of product to be released gradually to theaters.

Pictures such as *Rhapsody in Blue,* released in 1945, and *Devotion,* released in 1946 (both Warners films), had been made as long before as two, sometimes three, years.

Chronologically, the next film that Bergman made after *For Whom the Bell Tolls* was *Saratoga Trunk,* filmed in the spring of 1943. Prints of this picture were released for showing to the armed forces, but the civilian public did not see it until it was released on a limited basis in 1945, then put into general distribution in the spring of 1946. Meanwhile, Bergman had already made and appeared in three other films—*Gaslight, The Bells of St. Mary's, and Spellbound.* Despite Selznick's strong entreaties to the sales departments of the studios involved (MGM, RKO, and United Artists) to space the films out for maximum box-office impact, *The Bells of St. Mary's, Spellbound,* and *Saratoga Trunk* were released at the end of 1945, all within a month's time. "You know," ran a joke at the time, "I saw a picture today and Ingrid Bergman wasn't in it!" Selznick, thinking fast, declared 1945 "a Bergman year."

Another possible reason that Warners delayed release of *Saratoga Trunk* was that during its filming (in 1943), it occurred to the studio that the war-time public might not accept the picture, considering

SARATOGA TRUNK (1945). With Jerry Austin and Flora Robson.

it too frivolous, even, for non-musical escapist fare.

In any case, because *Saratoga Trunk* directly followed *For Whom the Bell Tolls* in Bergman's career, it is logical to consider it at this time.

From Paris to glittering New Orleans of the 1880s comes Clio Dulaine (Bergman), accompanied by Angélique (Flora Robson), her mulatto maid, and Cupidon (Jerry Austin), her manservant. Clio has sworn vengeance on the Dulaine family for depriving her of family rights because of her illegitimate birth. Her late mother was the mistress of Nicolas Dulaine, a wealthy man who died of a heart attack in her house on Rampart Street. Clio's mother was conveniently held responsible for her benefactor's death, and she, little Clio, and the servants, were banished to Paris. Now, Clio has come back to New Orleans to scandalize the Dulaines and thereby avenge her mother's honor and gain financial satisfaction.

Clio's plans are partially fulfilled when she meets Clint Maroon (Gary Cooper), a handsome Texas gambler who lives by his wits, but is fundamentally a man of good

SARATOGA TRUNK (1945). With Gary Cooper.

character as well as ambition. He is irresistibly drawn to Clio by her beauty and "steel-trap mind." Together, they go to find their fortunes at Saratoga Springs, a fashionable New York resort filled with "millionaires by the herds."

Posing as a French countess, and aided by the maneuverings of Mrs. Coventry Bellop (Florence Bates), an influential matchmaker, Clio becomes engaged to a young railroad tycoon, Bart Van Steed

(John Warburton). Clint takes an interest in Van Steed's struggle to hold onto the Saratoga Trunk, a valuable branch line that hauls coal from the Pennsylvania mines to the New England market. In the bloody battle of the finale, Clint saves Van Steed's railroad and wins Clio Dulaine as his wife.

Black-wigged and utterly bewitching, Bergman manages a personal triumph in—and over— *Saratoga Trunk*, a film that

58

sprawls, sags, and finally buckles under the weight of ponderous production, seemingly interminable length (two-and-a-quarter hours), and director Sam Wood's uncertainty as to what to make of Casey Robinson's overstuffed screenplay—a Gothic chiller, an engaging romantic trifle, an excursion into Edith Wharton's bustled world of ironic social comedy, or a two-fisted action picture. Given a grotesque retinue of a fiercely scowling, muttering mulatto maid in the unlikely person of a sooty, bandannaed Flora Robson, and Jerry Austin as a swarthy dwarf bodyguard prone to an excess of high spirits bordering on lunacy — and enough plot for half a dozen films — Bergman nevertheless creates a recognizably human and completely irresistible adventuress, and saves the picture from being a meticulously mounted exasperation.

Early on, we see Bergman seized with a frightening fit of hysterics (Robson smartly slaps her to her senses) over the odd appearance of a sofa in the eerie, decaying house on Rampart Street. Immediately afterwards, the dwarf howls "Blood up here!" from the bedroom above where, years before, Bergman's mother witnessed her lover's fatal

SARATOGA TRUNK (1945). With Flora Robson and Florence Bates.

heart attack. After the servants' gruesomely graphic account of her father's death (his blood, "spurting like the fountains of Versailles," stained the bedroom rug) and of her mother's attempted suicide, we are persuaded that a tale of terror is about to unfold.

No such thing. Soon, we are in the gay and colorful French Market quarter, where Bergman and Cooper first meet. From that point, it appears that an agreeable romantic story of flirtation between two likeable rogues is under way. Then, when the scene shifts to Saratoga, where we encounter a scheming social ogre, played to the nines by Florence Bates, we are in the midst of a gently mocking social satire of clannish millionaire dowagers who gather at the resort to gossip and to spoil reputations.

Finally, at the film's climax, we are suddenly in the midst of a bloody, action-packed brawl involving gangs of toughs who almost destroy the Saratoga Trunk Line. The dwarf is nearly killed in the brutal melee, and Cooper himself returns from it severely bruised and battered but sufficiently intact to claim Bergman for the final fadeout.

As diverting as the picture sounds, it is a giant jambalaya. The saving graces of Ferber's slight but juicy novel are its unpretentiousness and the author's skill in not letting her material bury her story. Wood, unfortunately, lets his embarrassment of riches—and the studio's property department—overwhelm him. The New Orleans and Saratoga settings are too ornately designed and too lovingly furnished, and the violent climactic sequences, including a spectacular train wreck, are protracted for the little they contribute to what seems chiefly to be, after all, a light period piece. One wonders why, since the release of the film was delayed for two years, the long interval was not used in judiciously pruning it.

Fresh from their no-nonsense roles in *For Whom the Bell Tolls*, Bergman and Cooper have a field day in *Saratoga Trunk*. Bergman catches exactly the engaging determination of the Creole bastard bent on avenging the wrongs done to her mother, and acquiring a husband, wealth, and social position. With her, we savor her sparring scenes with Bates, that splendid, slyly purring pussycat. (Bates' delivery of her amusing entrance line, as the rambunctious dwarf nearly knocks her down, "You *naughty* boy!" lingers fondly in the memory.) One also recalls with pleasure the scene in which Bergman voluptuously consumes fresh peaches bobbing in a glass of champagne ("That's the way Mama used to eat them in Paris. Delicious, and so cool"). Throughout, Bergman portrays a perfect hedonist and enters into her part with infectious gusto.

"Miss Bergman, become brunette and willful for this occasion, is magnificent," commented the *New York Herald Tribune* on her characterization, "playing with a verve and versatility that would make one think she actually was part Creole." *Time* magazine added that Bergman was "that rarity in Hollywood —a good-looking woman who can change her personality to suit her part. As Clio, freed from the virtuous nobility of her usual roles, her brilliant act of sexy razzle-dazzle makes most of Hollywood's glamor girls look like bobby-soxers."

The exchange of dialogue one relishes most is Bergman's supremely self-assured reply to a dazzled Curt Bois, who stammers, "You are—you are very beautiful." "Yes," chortles Bergman, every inch the movie goddess, "isn't it lucky?"

Gaslight, the film for which Ingrid Bergman won her first Academy Award, has a strange and tortuous history. British playwright Patrick Hamilton's melodrama had enjoyed success on the London stage as well as popularity as a 1939 British film with Diana Wynyard, Anton Walbrook, and Frank Pettingell. Transferred to Broadway late in 1941 as *Angel Street*, it starred Judith Evelyn, Vincent Price, and Leo G. Carroll, for a run of nearly thirteen hundred performances. Columbia Pictures bought the property for Irene Dunne, then sold it to MGM, who wanted it for Hedy Lamarr. One of the conditions of sale was that negatives of the British picture would be destroyed. When MGM's *Gaslight*, with Bergman, was released in Britain, its title there was *The Murder in Thornton Square*. Subsequently, surviving prints of Britain's own *Gaslight* have surfaced and have been shown occasionally in the United States under the title of *Angel Street*!

Whatever title it may go by, it is a crackling Victorian suspense thriller, filled with ingredients guaranteed to keep an audience's eyes glued to the characters and its heart in its mouth. When will the beautiful wife, blind with love, see her murderous mountebank of a husband, masquerading as a proper gentleman, for what he really is? In *Gaslight*, this question echoes and re-echoes through an overstuffed Victorian London townhouse, where pacing footsteps in the attic come like a thief in the night, and gas chandeliers suddenly—and unaccountably—burn low.

Once one has seen *Gaslight*, it is almost impossible to imagine anyone else in the roles that were played by Charles Boyer and Berg-

GASLIGHT (1944). With Charles Boyer.

man. He, suave and solicitous at first, then demonic, and at last cringing and contemptible. She, tremulous and vulnerable at first, then doubting her own sanity, and at last turning the tables triumphantly on the man who would destroy her. In describing her preparation for the role of a woman driven to the edge of madness, Bergman recalls that director George Cukor arranged for her to visit a mental hospital, where she was permitted to observe some of the patients. "One young woman

there interested me," she says, "and much of her strange qualities went into my characterization."

But Bergman and Boyer brought more than obvious blood-and-thunder theatrics to *Gaslight*. Cukor, who gave the film its inner pulse, sees to it that the theme — the kinds of love — is distinctly revealed in the way each of the two principals reacts in the presence of the beloved. For Bergman, it is love devoid of experience, as well as sexual dependence on a "matinee idol" husband. For Boyer, it is love of jewels. The expression of rapture on Boyer's face, seen in close-up, as he describes the crown jewels in the Tower of London, is, along with the scene in which he discovers the jewelry he has almost driven a woman to madness for, the only moment of real love in the film. Both Boyer and Cukor make these episodes memorable.

After knowing him only two weeks, lonely and impressionable Paula Alquist (Bergman) marries Gregory Anton (Boyer) a man much older than herself. Reluctantly, she agrees that they will take up residence in the house where one night as a child she had discovered her aunt strangled and the house turned upside down. It quickly becomes clear to us that Anton was the man who murdered the aunt and now is using his marriage to Paula as a means for leisurely exploring the attic of the house to find the jewels that had eluded him that night many years before. Night after night, on the pretext of going out, he ransacks the attic, making no attempt to hide from Paula the noise his search makes or the dimming of the gaslights in her room when he lights the attic burners to aid his search. He has cleverly prepared for Paula's noticing these things by "proving" she has forgotten where she put objects (he has surreptitiously removed them), and suggests she is in a sad state of increasing mental derangement, a condition, he tells Paula, that led to her own mother's death in a madhouse.

Circumstances arouse the curiosity of Scotland Yard's Brian Cameron (Joseph Cotten), who reopens the old case of unsolved murder. He suspects Anton is the murderer and questions his reasons for marrying young Paula. After allaying Paula's fears that she may be going insane by confirming the existence of sounds at the top of the house and the fading of gaslights, he confronts Anton and exposes him, just as Anton has found the jewels he sought, sewed onto a

GASLIGHT (1944). With Charles Boyer.

GASLIGHT (1944). With Joseph Cotten.

GASLIGHT (1944). With Charles Boyer.

stage costume Paula's aunt had worn in her greatest opera role. After Cameron ties Anton to a chair until the police come, he allows Paula an act of revenge on the man who so cruelly exploited her love and innocence. "Give me another chance," Anton pleads with Paula, "cut me free." Instead, she turns on him, saying "I hate you! Without a shred of pity, without a shred of regret, I watch you go with glory in my heart!"

Although *Gaslight* has attained the status of a minor classic film over the years, it was treated in a surprisingly offhand way by critics at the time of its release. All had praise for Bergman's stunning transformation from an infatuated child-woman to a woman of vengeance and for Boyer's icy suavity. They were delighted by Angela Lansbury's sullen, sluttish maid, Bronislau Kaper's eerie score introducing "The Last Rose of Summer" and the Mad Scene from *Lucia di Lammermoor,* and Cedric Gibbons and William Ferrari's wonderfully claustrophobic house in Thornton Square (they won the year's Art Direction Oscar), every square inch of which, it seems, is occupied by bibelots, furbelows, and gingerbread. (Edwin B. Willis and Paul Huldschinsky also won an Oscar for their set decoration.) And all were impressed by Cukor's guidance of Joseph Ruttenberg's camera, serpenting its way through the house, just as Anton coiled himself about Paula and the treasure to which she unwittingly held the key. But *The New York Times* expressed disappointment in "the very flexibility of the camera," saying that it omitted "much of the fearful immediacy of the play." Of Bergman and Boyer, it reported only that "these popular performers play their roles right to the hilt." The *New York Post* said that Bergman's "mingling of love, terror, and the growing sense of her own mind's failure represents one of the better achievements of the season."

Many comic relief moments stand out in the John Van Druten-Walter Reisch-John L. Balderston screenplay: Dame May Whitty's harmless old biddy who exclaims "Well!" at every turn of events; and, the best of them, the provocative singing of "Up in a Balloon, Boys" by Angela Lansbury (making her film debut), and her brazen self-advertisement to Anton: "I can take care of myself—when I want to."

In 1944, between completing *Gaslight* and beginning *Spellbound*, Bergman was asked by the U.S. Treasury Department to go on a national War Bond tour. By then, she, Dr. Lindstrom (now an M.D. at the Los Angeles County Hospital), and Pia had settled in a house in Beverly Hills. Back from Alaska, where she had entertained the troops, she set out to promote

With Leo McCarey and Dr. Peter Lindstrom, about to receive Oscar for GASLIGHT.

SPELLBOUND (1945).
As Dr. Constance Petersen.

the sale of bonds in cities across the country. On her return home in July, she began *Spellbound,* her second and last picture made directly under the personal supervision of David O. Selznick.

Ben Hecht freely adapted his screenplay for *Spellbound* from *The House of Dr. Edwardes,* a novel by Francis Beeding (the pseudonym of two authors). Nearly two hours in the telling, the film is not so much complex as it is prolix. Dr. Constance Petersen (Bergman) is a psychiatrist in a mental institution near Rutland, Vermont. Dr. Murchison (Leo G. Carroll), the

clinic's chief, is about to retire, and the staff awaits the arrival of his successor, Dr. Edwardes (Gregory Peck). Soon after the new supervisor presents himself at the hospital, Constance finds herself falling in love with the handsome young doctor.

But his clearly irrational fear of the sight of creases on white surfaces (tablecloths, robes, for example) suggests to Constance that although he may be a doctor, he is also a mentally disturbed stranger who has mysteriously assumed the identity of Dr. Edwardes. After Constance convinces "Dr. Edwardes" that he also has an amnesic condition probably arising from a guilt complex, he concludes that he must be wanted for the murder of the real Dr. Edwardes. A hunted man, he flees the clinic and goes to New York. Constance discovers his whereabouts in the city before pursuing police can apprehend them both.

She takes him to Rochester, in upstate New York, where Dr. Alex Brulov (Michael Chekhov), her former professor, can analyze the tormented man's dreams and find the reasons for his strange behavior. Brulov discovers that "J. B.," as Constance calls him, has felt responsible since childhood for his brother's accidental death by impalement on a fence. In addition, he is suffering from the shock of having witnessed Dr. Edwardes' death while skiing, which accounts for his violent antipathy toward white and any marks resembling ski tracks.

Back at the clinic, Constance learns from Dr. Murchison that he himself shot and killed Edwardes out of anger at being retired and replaced. After his confession, Constance coolly talks Murchison out of shooting her, whereupon the doctor, his fate sealed, turns the gun on himself. Now free of his anxieties, Dr. "J. B.," with Constance's devoted help, is ready to begin life anew.

"'The fault is not in our stars, but in ourselves ...' Shakespeare," runs the epigraph flashed on the screen at the beginning of *Spellbound*. One wonders if some other actor, maturer and with a more galvanizing personality than Gregory Peck had to offer at the time, might have made a more convincing bogus Dr. Edwardes. But Peck was a promising new Selznick star and he got the role. Although it is "J. B.'s" plight that makes the story, Bergman engages most of the viewer's attention. (Not surprisingly, she received the New York Film Critics' award as the Year's Best Actress.)

In addition to Peck's callow appearance and wooden acting, the film has other serious faults. One is its pretentious and simplistic

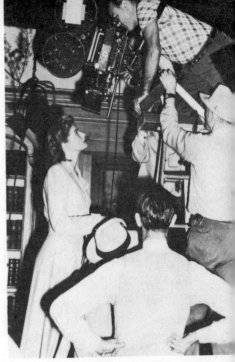

SPELLBOUND (1945).
Awaiting a camera setup.

"Freudian" dream sequence devised by surrealist painter Salvador Dali. Another is the "remarks-we-doubt-ever-got-made" nature of the dialogue. For example, in an early scene meant to establish Constance's professional credentials and character (she wears spectacles, so we *know* she's a bright girl), she reminds a colleague: "I have done a great deal of research on emotional problems and love difficulties." Later, "J.B." tells Constance that a mental patient in the hospital has just run amuck, tried to murder one of the

69

doctors, and then cut his own throat. "Is it bad?" Constance inquires. Still later, Constance turns on owlish old Dr. Brulov and says on "J. B.'s" behalf, "You don't know this man. You know only science. You know his mind but you don't know his heart." And towards the film's close, after two hours of guilt complex, misunderstanding, mayhem, murder, and suicide, Constance remarks, "Well, thank goodness it's all cleared up."

At another point, when she finds "J. B." in New York, we are shown a newspaper carrying the usual Hollywood banner headline concerned with that picture's plot, whatever else may be happening in the world that day: "Police Hunt Dr. Constance Petersen Believed Aiding Madman Wanted in Edwardes Mystery." As deft a summary of the plot till now as one could wish.

Bergman, making her first appearance in an Alfred Hitchcock thriller, does what she can — a great deal but not enough — to make credible a role requiring her to be alternately starchy and passionate. Peck, still an inexperienced actor at the time, betrays stage-fright paralysis, intimidated, perhaps, by the seasoned company of professionals he is thrust into. He underplays his role almost to the vanishing point.

On the credit side, *Spellbound* has several assets that make it still worth seeing. The first is Hitchcock and George Barnes' collaboration on some very striking photography. The flashback in which Peck relives the scene of his younger brother's gruesome death is visually exciting in its subjective, first-person point of view, and remains vividly in the memory long after much of the rest of the film has faded. Dali's surrealist dream, considered advanced in its time, is both dated art and psychology now, but it is interesting to see Hitchcock breaking away from the movies' usual smudged-focus idea of a dream and using the talents of an imaginative artist to depict one. A particularly effective scene takes place at the end; as Carroll trains the gun on Bergman (another first-person camera angle) we see a huge hand in the extreme foreground holding the weapon, turning slowly to keep Bergman in aim. Then, when she leaves the room, the gun turns toward its holder (that is to say, the audience) and fires pointblank at the camera in a subliminal Technicolor burst of red. Hitchcock admits that the isolated use of color was pure showmanship. It is effective, nevertheless, the rest of the film having accustomed the audience to a black-and-white world. (In television showings of *Spellbound*, this stunning device is regrettably lost.)

SPELLBOUND (1945). With Gregory Peck.

SPELLBOUND (1945). With Leo G. Carroll.

Not the least asset of the film is Miklos Rosza's imaginative score— lushly melodic and, when a theramin is employed, other-worldly. The composer deserved the Academy Award his score brought him.

To *The New York Times*, *Spellbound* was a "fine" and "rare" motion picture. Bergman's performance in it was a "guaranteed cure for what ails you, just as much as it is for Mr. Peck. It consists of her winning personality, softly but insistently suffused through a story of deep emotional content; of her ardent sincerity, her lustrous looks and her easy ability to toss off glibly a line of talk upon which most girls would choke." *Time* magazine took a sterner tone, saying that "the script allows Miss Bergman to do very little except tensely beg her lover to remember his boyhood. By flexing his jaw muscles and narrowing his eyes, Peck does his best to register the fact that all is not well with him . . . Again and again [Hitchcock] injects excitement into an individual scene with his manipulation of such trivia as a crack of light under a door, a glass of milk, or the sudden wailing of a locomotive whistle."

Probably Hitchcock himself sums up *Spellbound* best when he says of it today, "It's just another manhunt story wrapped up in pseudo-psychoanalysis."

With *Spellbound* completed at the end of September, 1944, Bergman again went on tours of military camps and hospitals and traveled with another bond-selling campaign. Then, in December, Selznick reluctantly loaned her to RKO to appear with Bing Crosby in *The Bells of St. Mary's*, director Leo McCarey and Crosby's successor to their enormously popular *Going My Way*, of the year before.

Because Selznick felt that sequels were rarely as good as the pictures that inspired them, that Bergman would merely stand around listening to Bing sing, and, most important, because no script had been written for him to approve, his terms for lending Bergman to RKO were demanding. He asked for and got the services of a top studio director, remake rights to *A Bill of Divorcement* and *Little Women* (both of which he had produced at RKO several years before), and $175,000 cash—a total value estimated at the time to be about half a million dollars.

Production on *The Bells of St. Mary's* began in February of the following year, with a script by Dudley Nichols, based on an idea by McCarey, and photography by George Barnes, whose work on *Rebecca* and *Spellbound* had delighted Selznick. Bergman's answer to Selznick's misgivings was to endow the role of Sister Bene-

THE BELLS OF ST. MARY'S (1945). With Joan Carroll.

73

dict, a part dipped in equal parts of sugar and spice, with warmth and humor.

James Agee, an articulate critic for *The Nation*, writing soon after the film opened in early December, 1945, was among the critics who found themselves immune to the sure-fire appeal of some of the picture's situations: "I find very objectionable the movies' increasing recognition of the romantic-commercial values of celibacy. I like hardly better a little boxing lesson in which Mother Bergman shows one of the schoolboys how not to lead with the other cheek. I am just plain horrified by the way in which the sisters hound an old nabob into beneficence." By contrast, the *New York Herald Tribune* rejoiced in the picture's "sincerity, feeling, and artistry." The *Times* felt that "the whole story-line developed toward the wheedling of a building for the school ... is unconvincing and vaguely immoral.... There are moments (not the close-up shot of her praying) in which [Bergman] glows with tenderness and warmth."

The slender plot of the film involves the differing philosophies of Father Chuck O'Malley (Crosby, re-creating the character in *Going My Way*) and Sister Mary Benedict (Bergman), the Sister Superior of a New York parochial school housed in a decaying building. The priest,

assigned to the nun's parish, is easy-going ("If you're ever in trouble, dial O for O'Malley"), feeling that man's innate goodness will carry the day. The sister, on the other hand, believes that kindly but firm discipline is what is needed to turn youngsters into good Christians and citizens. Their approaches to education eventually reconciled, together they persuade a Scrooge-like industrialist (Henry Travers) to part with a new building that will better accommodate Sister Benedict's school. A victim of tuberculosis, the nun is forced to retire, but she finds comfort and reward for her labors in the love her pupils bear her, and the ungrudging admiration of Father O'Malley. During the course of the film, Crosby sings "Aren't You Glad You're You?", "The Bells of St. Mary's," and "Ave Maria," and Bergman sings a Swedish song, "It's Spring."

During the filming of the movie, Bergman won an Oscar for her performance in *Gaslight*, Crosby received one for his acting in *Going My Way*, and McCarey was similarly rewarded for his direction of the latter picture. On the *Bells of St. Mary's* set the day after the presentation ceremonies, the three were toasted and feted. "I thought I could never be so happy again," Bergman said later of the occasion.

The critics notwithstanding, *The*

With director Leo McCarey, Bing Crosby, and Property Man George Gabe, celebrating Crosby's birthday.

THE BELLS OF ST. MARY'S (1945). With Henry Travers and Ruth Donnelly.

Bells of St. Mary's was an enormous hit when it was released the following Christmas, and the fact that it boasted three major Academy Award winners resulted, contrary to Selznick's wariness, in its doing even better business than *Going My Way.*

Although Bergman played an adventuress in *Saratoga Trunk,* and was to play women of flexible morals in *Notorious* and *Arch of Triumph,* and a murderess in *Under Capricorn,* the image of virginal purity that she projected so convincingly as Sister Benedict stamped itself indelibly on the public mind as the "real" Ingrid Bergman. It was a heavy halo that was soon to slip from her head.

Bergman's final picture for Selznick was *Notorious.* Their association had lasted seven years and brought eleven films to the screen. The producer's stable of Selznick International stars—including Joan Fontaine, Joseph Cotten, Gregory Peck, Dorothy McGuire, Alida Valli, and Louis Jourdan— had gone or were soon to go their separate ways. Jennifer Jones, who became Mrs. David O. Selznick in 1949, continued to make pictures under her husband's supervision until 1961.

No longer having his own studio in which to produce his films, Selznick assembled a cast, director, and screenwriter for *Notorious* and sold them to RKO as a "package." Bergman's costar was Cary Grant, who had been nominated for an Oscar as Best Actor (for *None But the Lonely Heart*) the same year the actress won hers for *Gaslight.* The film marked several reunions: Claude Rains was cast with Bergman for the first time since *Casablanca,* her director was again—this time with happier results—Alfred Hitchcock, and for *Notorious,* Ben Hecht provided a tighter screenplay than he had for *Spellbound.*

Over the years, *Notorious* has won a favored place in the affections of Bergman, Grant, and Hitchcock admirers. Some consider it the actress' best picture; others place it just after *Casablanca.* Hecht's taut and sophisticated script (on which Hitchcock collaborated) gave the cast all the room it needed to display its various special talents. From Grant, *Notorious* elicited one of his most pungent characterizations, as a cynical but romantically vulnerable American intelligence agent. For Hitchcock, the film's swiftly paced story offered an ideal chance to display his genius for intrigue, danger, and sudden plot turns—combining sex and suspense. Rains' role as a rich and powerful Nazi schemer allowed him to be both despicable yet oddly sympathetic. As a playgirl with a compliant and amorous dis-

76

NOTORIOUS (1946). With Cary Grant.

position, but whose ethical convictions are unshakeable, Bergman gives one of her best performances.

Bitterly disillusioned and inclined to drink too much, Alicia Huberman (Bergman) is the daughter of a convicted Nazi spy. Devlin (Grant), an American spy, contacts Alicia to make use of her knowledge of Nazi inner circles in uncovering a mysterious plan being hatched by a band of Nazi refugees in postwar Rio de Janeiro. Alicia accepts Devlin's proposition as a chance to prove she is a good American and to right her father's wrongs. Before long, Alicia and Devlin are having a casual love affair.

To discover the plotters' secret Alicia must seduce Alexander Sebastian (Rains), a prominent local Nazi who was a friend of her father. Alicia, suspecting that Devlin loves her, expects him to forbid her going to such an extreme. But because Devlin is not convinced of *her* feelings, he says nothing, and she goes ahead with the plan, partly in anger at Devlin and partly to help the mission. Soon, Sebastian falls in love with Alicia and asks her to marry him. Again she hopes that Devlin will try to dissuade her; and again Devlin, assuming that a wealthy marriage is just what an adventuress would want, encourages her to accept Sebastian's proposal as an ideal means of uncovering the plot.

The Sebastians give a gala party after their wedding and Alicia passes Devlin the key to Sebastian's wine cellar, where they find particles of uranium ore in the bottles. Sebastian discovers them and realizes that they are American spies and that they have found the damning evidence of the Nazis' plot to manufacture atomic weapons for another war. Sebastian's mother (German actress Leopoldine Konstantin, billed here as Madame Konstantin) demands that her son murder Alicia by gradually poisoning her. Devlin allows his love for Alicia to jeopardize the success of their mission by invading the Sebastian house to rescue her. Sebastian, to save his beloved Alicia, allows them to escape and in a grim closing scene, it is suggested that he will be killed by his colleagues for his treachery. The atomic plot exposed, Alicia and Devlin are now able to marry, free of their misconceptions about each other.

When the film opened in August, 1946, *The New York Times* called *Notorious* a "taut, superior film," adding that "Mr. Hecht and Mr. Hitchcock have done a forthright and daring thing: they have made the girl, played by Miss Bergman, a lady of notably loose morals....There is nothing unreal or puritanical in [Bergman and

NOTORIOUS (1946). With Claude Rains and Cary Grant.

Grant's] exposure of a frank, grown-up amour. And [they] have played it with surprising and disturbing clarity .... Mr. Grant, who is exceptionally solid, is matched for acting honors in the cast by Claude Rains ... [whose] shrewd and tense performance of this invidious character is responsible for much of the anguish that the situation creates. ... A splendid touch of chilling arrogance as a German mother is added by Madame Konstantin." In *The Nation*, James Agee wrote, "I think that Ingrid Bergman's performance here is the best of hers that I have seen."

There are several scenes in *Notorious* that filmgoers remember with undimmed delight. One of them is "the longest kiss in history," as advertising copy for the picture described it. It begins on the balcony of Grant's hotel suite, overlooking Rio, moves inside, continues as they cross the room. Grant even talks on the telephone, interrupting the kissing only with an exchange of domestic dialogue about their chicken dinner and who will wash the dishes afterwards. As a spoof of the usual clutch-and-kiss love scene, it deserves its celebrity. This scene and the one in which Alicia hesitantly tells Devlin about Sebastian's proposal ("He wants to marry me"), are remarkable more for what they suggest than what they show. Bergman and Grant generate between them an erotic

NOTORIOUS (1946). With Madame Konstantin and Claude Rains.

NOTORIOUS (1946). With Cary Grant.

tension that had not been felt in Bergman's films since the Bogart-Bergman combination in *Casablanca*.

Another memorable moment comes during the elaborate party. Hitchcock (with the able assistance of his cameraman, Ted Tetzlaff) has the camera slowly descend from high above the great foyer of the house, float down past a grand chandelier, show the milling guests below with Bergman in their midst. The others stroll away and as the camera continues to descend, it moves in for a closeup of Bergman's left hand nervously clasping and unclasping the key to the all-important wine cellar.

Still another tense and powerful scene is the one in which Sebastian, a man of great personal authority, is bent to the will of his even more dominating mother to admit that his love for Alicia is far less important than the danger that her discovery in the cellar has placed them. Rains' depiction of a man torn desperately between love for his wife and acceptance of the fact that he must nevertheless destroy her is a truly moving performance.

Hitchcock enjoys telling the story about how, when he first had the idea for the picture in 1944 (it began shooting in September, 1945), he had by pure chance decided to make uranium the secret substance in the wine bottles. In his researches into the matter, his innocent inquiries to officials and scientists as to whether that rare element could possibly be relevant to atomic weapons were met with stunned silence. The FBI, fearing a leak from the top-secret Manhattan Project, which was developing the atomic bomb, kept Hitchcock under surveillance for several weeks. Off to this propitious start, the picture more than fulfilled its promise as espionage entertainment of the first order.

Notorious not only marked Bergman's last film under her contract with Selznick, it was also her last successful movie for ten years.

As *Notorious* went into production, rumors were spreading that "all was not well" with Dr. and Mrs. Lindstrom. Each was a dedicated professional — Bergman working long hard hours at the studio and Lindstrom working long hard hours at the hospital. In addition, while he preferred a reclusive life in his spare time, she enjoyed meeting and mixing with friends and making new acquaintances.

After completing *Notorious* in November of 1945, Bergman took a vacation in New York to shop, see plays and movies, and visit old friends, including Kay Brown, who had been instrumental in bringing Bergman to America. One of the pictures the actress saw that fall of

With Dr. Peter Lindstrom in July, 1946.

1945 was entitled *Open City*. A semi-documentary filmed under primitive wartime conditions, it depicted with lacerating honesty what Italians had suffered under the German occupation of Italy during the war years. Directed by then relatively unknown Roberto Rossellini, the picture was hailed as a rawly realistic masterpiece and a film of such overwhelming impact that it gave viewers the impression they were seeing the film medium born anew. Bergman must have felt that something fresh and vital

was blowing in the wind when, after *Open City* was over, she exclaimed to her companion, "Christ, what an experience!" Deeply impressed, she was soon to meet the creator of that most un-Hollywood film.

Meanwhile, having rejected Selznick's offer of a new seven-year contract, Bergman exercised her new-found freedom. Bergman and Lindstrom decided that she would star, and accept a 25 percent interest in, a screen version of Erich Maria Remarque's current bestseller, *Arch of Triumph*. Produced by a new company, Enterprise Studios, the picture had a promising lineup of names, principally that of Charles Boyer, her costar in *Gaslight*. In addition to prestigious supporting actors Charles Laughton and Louis Calhern, it would be directed by Lewis Milestone, who had guided the classic 1930 film version of Remarque's novel, *All Quiet on the Western Front*.

What could possibly go wrong? Starting from the time it began shooting in June 1946, practically everything. Enterprise proceeded to sink under the weight of heavy production costs, script indecisions —the credits ultimately went to Milestone and Harry Brown—and the seeming inability on anyone's part to stop filming more and more footage. (It was finally edited down to two hours.) For the present at least the public was tired of war films and despite its cast, director, and cost, *Arch of Triumph* lost over $2 million. It was Bergman's first American failure.

To call *Arch of Triumph* turgid is to endow it with a sparkle wholly absent from it. A movie of nearly unrelieved talkiness and drabness, it is set in Paris just prior to World War II, against a background of the growing Nazi threat throughout Europe. By a chance encounter, Ravic (Boyer), a surgeon and anti-

ARCH OF TRIUMPH (1948).
As Joan Madou.

Nazi underground worker, prevents Joan Madou (Bergman), a lonely and disillusioned demimondaine, from jumping into the Seine. (To depict Joan's utter depravity, the director pulled out all the stops by having Bergman smoke onscreen.) The doctor gets her a job singing at the Scheherazade cabaret, where his old Russian friend, a former military officer under the Czar, is now doorman (Calhern). Joan and Ravic fall in love. When Ravic encounters Haake (Laughton), the Nazi official

Celebrating Bergman and Charles Boyer's birthdays on the set, with director Lewis Milestone (left), Boyer, and Enterprise Studio executives.

ARCH OF TRIUMPH (1948). With Charles Boyer.

who was responsible for the death of Ravic's fiancée, he kills him. Meanwhile, despite her happiness as his mistress, Joan has reverted to her old ways and has begun an affair with a wealthy man (Stephen Bekassy). When her new lover finds that he shares Joan's love with Ravic, he shoots her. Evidently, the point is being made that the moral apathy of such as Joan Madou will cause Paris to fall before the Nazis, and the strength and courage of such as Ravic will resist and conquer them.

The critics were almost uniformly inhospitable to Enterprise's maiden voyage. *The New York Times* called it "a gold-plated, Chanel-perfumed version of down-at-heels boy-meets-girl.... From within Lewis Milestone's roving camera, we watch love as it is made by two of the movies' most able craftsmen, repetitiously and at exceeding length. ... Laughton is absurd as the Nazi brute." The *New York Herald Tribune* observed that "Boyer overdoes the taciturn, eyebrow-raising, secretive refugee ... [Bergman's] lithe performance, always a notch or two above realism, makes him appear bored."

Although Enterprise Studios had other projects in view—a film to return Garbo to the screen and an adaptation of Stendhal's *Charterhouse of Parma* with Marlon Brando—none of them came into being, for *Arch of Triumph* was the organization's first and last cinema venture.

As *Arch of Triumph* neared completion in September of 1946, Bergman was approached by the Playwrights Company, a group including dramatists Maxwell Anderson, Robert E. Sherwood, Elmer Rice, and composer Kurt Weill, to star in a Broadway production of Anderson's new play, *Joan of Lorraine*. Because enacting the Maid represented the fulfillment of a dream that Bergman had cherished for many years, and because of Anderson's reputation as a leading American playwright, Bergman accepted without seeing the script. A play about actors engaged in a contemporary production dealing with the historical Maid, *Joan of Lorraine* was written with a purpose described by Anderson himself: "The problem of what to believe, and how man defends his belief in a world of power politics and disillusionment, is hard to write about directly, but it's not a new problem. It was Socrates' torment, and Lincoln's, and Joan of Arc's, and many others. I chose Joan because she lived far from our times, and the scenes from her life would offer a complete contrast with the rehearsal— would give the actors a real chance to make a new world and set it down on a bare stage."

JOAN OF ARC (1948).
As the Maid of Orleans.

For Bergman, her supporting cast, Anderson, and the producing company, *Joan of Lorraine* was a great triumph when it opened at the Alvin Theatre in New York on November 18, 1946. Simply, the play tells the story of an actress, Mary Grey (Bergman), and her eventual acceptance of the need for compromise on small details in interpreting certain episodes in the life of Joan of Arc in order to achieve the larger truths of the Maid's spiritual significance. Brooks Atkinson in *The New York Times* said, "Miss Bergman adds frankness, force, and light that comes out of her own wealth of perception, and hers is the Joan of religious inspiration and fable."

In the spring of the following year, at the end of the play's seven-month limited run, Bergman was awarded the Antoinette Perry Award and the Drama League of New York's Gold Medal for the year's most distinguished stage performance. On presenting that award to Bergman at the formal ceremonies, Helen Hayes said, "We thank you, Miss Bergman, for bringing the theater back to Broadway."

Inevitably, in the wake of *Joan of Lorraine*'s success, Bergman decided to bring her conception of the Maid of Orleans to the screen. Although Maxwell Anderson wrote, with Andrew Solt, the

JOAN OF ARC (1948). At Joan's trial.

screenplay for the film, called *Joan of Arc*, it was unwisely decided to depart from the play's fascinating then-and-now time scheme and to present instead a straightforward historical treatment of the girlhood of Joan, her trial, and her martyrdom. Backed by a business partnership including herself, her husband, producer Walter Wanger, and Victor Fleming (who had directed Bergman in *Dr. Jekyll and Mr. Hyde*), filming began, after nearly a year of intensive preparation, in January, 1948. Large and elaborate interior sets and sprawling exteriors were built at the Hal Roach Studio, not far from the old Selznick studios where Bergman had begun her American film career ten years before. With its many sets, thousands of costumes and props, an enormous cast, and the added complications of Technicolor photography, it is not surprising to learn that the film cost $5 million — $1 million more than Fleming's earlier *Gone With the Wind*.

The story of *Joan of Arc* (released through RKO) followed the familiar path of historical fact—from the voices the young girl hears, through her pleas to the Dauphin Charles VII to let her fight the English invaders, her victory at Orleans, Charles' coronation at Rheims, to her capture, trial, and

JOAN OF ARC (1948). As the martyred Joan.

execution by the British and the corrupt clergy.

For the greater part of its two-and-a-half hour length, *Joan of Arc* presents many stirring sequences of pageantry. But too much of the film is merely empty spectacle and almost comic-strip progression from one historical highlight to the next. Where Anderson had provided an intellectually provocative, if not classic, play in *Joan of Lorraine*, the script for the film offers long stretches of flat, banal, and uninspired dialogue. Laurence Olivier's thrilling "Once more unto the breach, dear friends, once more," before the Battle of Agincourt in the brilliant 1946 production of Shakespeare's *Henry V* still rang in movie audience's ears; Bergman had only an unreverberating "Forward!" with which to exhort her French soldiers into immortality.

Most of the critics admired Bergman's fortitude in the face of certain disaster, understandably confusing the actress' fate with that of the Saint's. When the picture opened in November 1948, *The New York Times* reflected the general feeling when it conceded that "pictorially, it is one of the most magnificent films ever made," but concluded that "the mystery, the meaning, and magnificence of the poor girl called Joan have just been missed."

Although she had recently enjoyed great success on Broadway, Bergman had just been in two badly received movies. (*Joan of Arc*, although harshly treated by the critics, was widely attended, particularly in Europe.) Then, while vacationing in New York in the spring of 1948, she saw *Paisan*, Rossellini's sequel to *Open City*, which dramatized events in the German retreat through Italy. Again, she was struck by the power and directness of the Italian's filmmaking. If this was to be the film style of the future, she reasoned, it would be best to involve herself with it as quickly as possible.

In a widely quoted letter to Rossellini, Bergman acknowledged her fascination with his films and expressed a hope that she might join him in a motion picture venture: "If you need a Swedish actress who speaks English very well, who has not forgotten her German, who is not very understandable in French and who in Italian knows only 'ti amo' [words she had spoken in *Arch of Triumph*], I am ready to come and make a film with you." Rossellini cabled a reply expressing his gratitude for her compliments and interest, and thus began one of the most publicized liaisons—connubial as well as artistic—of the time.

It is true that Bergman was discouraged with her Hollywood

career, that her new film, *Under Capricorn*, soon to be made in London with Alfred Hitchcock directing, was nothing about which she was very excited, and that she and Peter Lindstrom had continued to drift further and further apart. It was also true, however, that her letter to Rossellini was hardly the open flirtation it has seemed in retrospect (and that Rossellini himself may have interpreted it as being), but an earnest application for serious film work from a dedicated actress. In any case, in the summer of 1948, Bergman began work on *Under Capricorn*. During filming, she, her husband, and Rossellini met weekends in Paris to discuss plans for *After the Storm* (retitled *Stromboli*), the picture she hoped to make with the Italian director.

Released in the fall of 1949, *Under Capricorn* proved to be one of Bergman's (and Hitchcock's) least successful films. Set in Sydney, Australia, in 1831, its plot is a fustian, unconvincing mixture of hard-breathing melodrama and romance. Charles Adare (Michael Wilding), cousin of the governor (Cecil Parker), is newly arrived from Ireland to seek his fortune. He is invited to dinner by Sam Flusky (Joseph Cotten), a former convict and "financial genius" who is now the wealthy husband of Charles' cousin, Henrietta (Berg-

man). At the Flusky household, Charles finds that Henrietta is an alcoholic. The slyly domineering housekeeper, Milly (Margaret Leighton), who is secretly in love with her master, terrorizes her mistress. In undertaking to restore his cousin's health and self-confidence, Charles falls in love with her. Sam, inflamed by Milly's insinuations, provokes a fight in which Charles is accidentally wounded. Henrietta then admits to Charles that she is guilty of murdering her brother in Ireland years before, the crime for which her husband was convicted and transported. Charles renounces his love for Henrietta, but before returning to Ireland, he exposes Milly as a conniving hypocrite.

"There wasn't enough humor in the film," Hitchcock has said of *Under Capricorn*. (*Intended* humor may have been absent, but such lines as Wilding's "Come away, come away from all this," breathed into Bergman's ear, were certainly good for a laugh.) Mainly the film suffered by having both not enough of anything and too much of everything. There was not enough tension and genuine suspense; not enough sense of real place, despite elaborate miniature work and stunning special effects depicting Sydney harbor; too much stifling studio atmosphere (even in exterior scenes, one has no feeling of actu-

UNDER CAPRICORN (1949). With Joseph Cotten and Cecil Parker.

ally being outdoors), and too much shouting and posturing. It is the kind of insubstantial meringue that was responsible, in part at least, for sending Bergman off to fresh breezes in Southern Italy and Rossellini's gritty neorealism.

The picture begins promisingly. Wilding's cocky nonchalance is pleasantly reminiscent of Errol Flynn, as he insinuates himself into the Flusky household. Cotten is intriguingly brisk and brooding in his establishing scenes, but his characterization soon becomes unvaryingly morose and expressionless. Bergman's Ophelia-like entrance at the dinner party is

exquisitely handled and her appearance is nicely shocking— she looks convincingly drawn, diffident, and deathly. But after introducing her as far from a well lady, her makeup too suddenly reverts to idealized Bergman, a perfect specimen of blooming health.

At intervals, Hitchcock borrows the technique of lengthy takes he used in *Rope* but here he seems concerned merely with avoiding cutting from face to face. Two examples stand out: Bergman's powerfully acted confession of murder to Wilding; and the seemingly nonstop monologue that Leighton (cast as cat to Bergman's

UNDER CAPRICORN (1949). With Margaret Leighton and Joseph Cotten.

UNDER CAPRICORN (1949). With Joseph Cotten and Michael Wilding.

canary—one can almost see the feathers around her mouth) addresses to Cotten while Bergman and Wilding are at the governor's ball. These scenes distract as feats of the performers' endurance instead of drawing the audience deeper into the drama.

Despite Bergman's characteristic total commitment to her role, it is really Wilding's light-hearted and likeable performance, Parker's fussy fuming as the governor, and Leighton's unfortunately much-too-Mayfair speech and manner that remain, for better and worse, in the memory. The sets for the Fluskys' house, called with uncanny aptness, "Why Weepest Thou?" are an interior decorator's dream. The film, for all its intended Gothic mood and substance, is too creamily pretty. Jack Cardiff's muted Technicolor photography is rich and restrained, but it is inappropriate to a film that tried to repeat the haunting formula of *Rebecca*. Critically and financially, *Under Capricorn* was Bergman's third disappointment in a row.

In January 1949, *Paisan* received the New York Film Critics' award as Best Foreign Language Picture of the Year. After personally accepting the honor in New York, Rossellini flew to Los Angeles for further discussion about Bergman's next film, staying with the Lindstroms in their guest house in Beverly Hills. "Hollywood is like a factory that turns out fine sausages," he observed, adding, "I cannot work here. I go back to Italy where I have freedom." At the end of February, Rossellini returned to Italy. On March 20, Bergman joined him in Rome. Hordes of reporters and photographers were at the airport to document the star's arrival. Rossellini met her and escorted her to her suite at Rome's elegant Excelsior Hotel. Bergman's search for new challenges had begun.

Bergman's association with Rossellini rocked the film world—and the world at large—to its foundations. That the beloved nun of *The Bells of St. Mary's* and Joan of Arc should abandon husband and daughter, not to mention Hollywood itself, to dally with an Italian unknown to the general American public was unforgivable. Nothing illustrates more vividly the barrage of violent criticism that resulted from her falling in love with Roberto Rossellini than the diatribe that Edwin C. Johnson, then the senior Senator from Colorado, delivered from the floor of the Senate. For an hour, he fulminated against Bergman as a "free-love cultist," a "powerful influence for evil," and "Hollywood's apostle of degradation." Every cloud has its silver lining, however, for he expressed the hope that "out of her ashes may come a better Hollywood." The bigger the idol, the more resounding the fall.

Selznick himself admitted that he was responsible for Bergman's public image as "Saint Ingrid": "I hired a press agent who was an expert at shielding stars from the press, and we released only stories that emphasized her sterling character. We deliberately built her up as the normal, healthy, non-neurotic career woman devoid of scandal and with an idyllic home life. I guess that backfired later."

CHAPTER III

THE YEARS WITH ROSSELLINI

Stromboli, terra di Dio (Stromboli, God's Earth, the picture's full title) was filmed during the spring and summer of 1949. It tells the story of Karin (Bergman), a Lithuanian refugee from a World War II internment camp, who goes to Stromboli with her young fisherman husband (Mario Vitale). Unable to establish a rapport with the island natives, she desperately tries to escape, even though she is pregnant. After a violent eruption of Stromboli's volcano, she reaches the port on the other side of the island, but becomes lost and falls asleep. Upon awakening, she invokes God to help her. "I can't go back," she cries.

When the picture was released in New York in February 1950, *The New York Times* expressed nearly everyone's disappointment in the new film by the creator of *Open City* and *Paisan*: "Some share of the responsibility may be borne by its distributor, RKO. For, to add to the mystery and confusion already surrounding this film is the rumor that considerable re-editing was done in Hollywood....A strange listlessness and incoherence is perceptible through the whole film, as

STROMBOLI (1950). Between camera setups.

STROMBOLI (1950). With Mario Vitale.

With Roberto Rossellini.

Ernest Hemingway, Gary Cooper, and David O. Selznick and his wife, Jennifer Jones.

A week after the birth of Robertino, Bergman obtained a Mexican divorce from Peter Lindstrom, and a few days later she and Rossellini were married by proxy in Juarez, Mexico. (Rossellini had, in his turn, obtained an annulment of his previous marriage, on the grounds that he had married under the influence of drugs.) Dr. Lindstrom was given custody of Pia, then twelve, and Bergman was granted permission to see her daughter during Pia's school vacations.

In June 1952, Bergman bore her husband twin daughters, Isotta and Isabella. By now, a matron and mother of three children by her second union, Bergman won a certain grudging respect from many of the people who had at first been most appalled by her actions.

The Rossellinis continued to make their films. Ironically, except for the crudity of much of the photography (harsh black-and-white contrasts, graininess, obvious and distracting dubbed dialogue), which had been appropriate to his earlier semidocumentary pictures, the new films were not so very different from the conventional Hollywood product that Bergman had rebelled against: tear-jerking dramas of brave women standing alone against brutal forces of the

though it had been dreamed up and put together not by masters but by earnest amateurs."

In February 1950, Bergman gave birth to a son by Rossellini, Robertino. The Bergman-Rossellini scandal broke out afresh. What more proof was needed that the lovers were flaunting their affair? However, friends like Charles Boyer and Cary Grant sent her congratulatory cables. Grant's, for example, said: "Ingrid dearest: It would not be possible in a single cablegram to tell you of all your friends who send you love and affection." Other similar communications came from Helen Hayes, John Steinbeck,

EUROPA '51 (The Greatest Love) *(1951). With Alexander Knox.*

world. In fact, they were similar in content to the *pre*-Hollywood films she had made in Sweden, nearly twenty years before. Bergman, it was becoming apparent, was not another Anna Magnani; Rossellini was not a new Curtiz, Cukor, or Hitchcock.

Toward the end of 1951, Bergman costarred with Alexander Knox in *Europa '51* (*The Greatest Love*), shown in the United States early in 1954. It is a gloomy drama of a woman who tries to commit herself to a life of selfless dedication after her son dies. She is finally sent to an asylum by her husband and family when she tries to help a bandit escape from the police. *The New York Times* sympathized with Bergman when it reviewed "this dismal and dolorous account.... [She] deserves something better— much better—for her next time around."

Her next film for Rossellini was

SIAMO DONNE (We, the Women, "Ingrid Bergman") (1953). With the hungry hen.

1953's "Ingrid Bergman," a twenty-minute episode in a five-part omnibus called *Siamo donne (We, the Women)*. In this domestic vignette, Bergman (playing herself) tries to save her rose bushes from the ravages of a hungry hen. She cages the fowl and tries to make her dog eat it. The bird is saved at the last moment. Bergman spends much of her time in this film screaming angrily in fluent Italian.

In *Viaggio in Italia (Journey to Italy)*, also made in 1953, Bergman and George Sanders (the romantic pair of *Rage in Heaven*) play a quiet British couple who have come to Naples to dispose of property left

them by a relative. While Bergman goes sightseeing, Sanders becomes bored and restless and decides to divorce his wife. But during a religious procession they witness, the couple is moved to reconcile their differences. (The French film magazine *Cahiers du Cinema* listed *Viaggio in Italia* as one of the ten great films of all time. Few viewers share this enthusiasm.) A shortened version of this picture was released in the United States in 1955, as *Strangers*.

In 1953 and 1954, Bergman appeared in Rossellini's stage production of Arthur Honegger's 1938 dramatic oratorio, *Jeanne d'Arc au bûcher (Joan of Arc at the Stake)*, set to words by Paul Claudel. Bergman performed the dramatic, spoken role of Joan in a fully staged version with scenery and costumes. Performed at La Scala, Milan; at the San Carlo Opera, Naples; the Stockholm Opera; the Paris Opera; the Barcelona Opera; the Stoll Theatre, London; and in a concert performance broadcast by the BBC, the production was eventually filmed in 1954, in color, and distributed in Europe under its Italian title, *Giovanna d'Arco al rogo*.

Because the Bergman-Rossellini artistic collaboration had not resulted in any commercially successful films, money to continue financing them was becoming

VIAGGIO IN ITALIA (Journey to Italy; Strangers) *(1954). With George Sanders.*

GIOVANNA D'ARCO AL ROGO (Joan of Arc at the Stake) *(1954). On the set with Rossellini.*

ANGST (Fear) (1955). With Kurt Kreuger.

increasingly difficult to raise. Their final movie together was a German-language production made in Munich in the autumn of 1954. Based on a story by Stefan Zweig, *Angst (Fear)* centers on a rich industrialist's adulterous wife, who is being blackmailed. When she discovers that the blackmailer is working on instructions from her husband, shame and despair cause her to contemplate suicide. Instead, she finds reason for living, in the company of her children.

During the filming of *Angst*, Dr. Lindstrom, by now a well-known brain surgeon, married a professional colleague, Dr. Agnes Ronanek, in Pittsburgh. A son, Peter Michael, was born in 1956.

Early in 1955, Angelo Solmi, one of Italy's most respected film critics, addressed an open letter to the Rossellinis begging them to depart the movie scene while they still had some dignity left to them. Writing in the influential weekly, *Oggi*, he said: "After half a dozen [films] with negative results it confirms the inability of the couple to create anything acceptable to the public or the critics. Once the world's indisputable No. 1 star and successor to Greta Garbo, Miss

ELENA ET LES HOMMES (Paris Does Strange Things) *(1956). With Mel Ferrer.*

ELENA ET LES HOMMES (Paris Does Strange Things) *(1956). With Jean Marais and Mel Ferrer.*

Bergman in recent pictures has been only a shadow of herself."

Later that year, Jean Renoir, the distinguished French director of such classics as *Grand Illusion* and *Rules of the Game*, asked Bergman to come to Paris to star in a film that he had written especially for her, *Elena et les hommes (Paris Does Strange Things)*. The money was attractive and Bergman accepted, with her husband's permission. Filmed in Technicolor, it is a light, gay period piece set in Paris in the 1880s, in which Princess Elena (Bergman) meets Henri (Mel Ferrer), who introduces her to General Rolland (Jean Marais), the minister of war. Attracted to the General, Elena uses her charms to inspire him to acquire greater political glory. Being fickle, she shifts her romantic attention back to Henri, and the General abandons his plans to seize power. Though it strives to be an opulently mounted social satire, *Paris Does Strange Things* was obviously made on a less-than-opulent budget. A parade, for example, shows mostly reaction shots of the crowd, not the parade itself. Bergman is again lovely to behold in color and becoming costumes, but her only good line is her retort to a woman plainly impressed by the fact that Elena is a princess. "In Poland," Bergman says airily, "there are lots of princesses."

Renoir disavows the edited version that Warner Brothers released in New York in March, 1957—after Bergman had won an Academy Award for *Anatasia* (made after the Renoir film). *The New York Times* wrote: "It appears that M. Renoir was undecided whether this was a romantic drama or a slapstick farce, so the actors give it to him both ways, indiscriminately and at the top of their lungs. ... The one clue to why this strange concoction was hastily booked at the Paramount is that Miss Bergman just won an Oscar. She should use it to hit somebody over the head."

While making the Renoir film, Bergman was approached with an offer to appear in either Tennessee Williams' *Cat on a Hot Tin Roof* or Robert Anderson's *Tea and Sympathy* on the Paris stage. The actress rejected the role in the Williams play as being too young for her, accepting instead the part of Laura Reynolds, the middle-aged woman in *Tea and Sympathy* who initiates a shy adolescent into the mysteries of sex. Although she could speak French well, Bergman requested nearly a year to learn the part and perfect her French.

While Bergman was studying her role in *Tea and Sympathy*, her life took a dramatic turn. Twentieth Century-Fox had acquired the film rights to *Anastasia*, the stage success adapted by Guy Bolton from a play by Marcelle Maurette, and planned a spectacular color production, in Cinemascope, with a cast to include Yul Brynner and Helen Hayes. Bergman's old friend and mentor, Kay Brown, arrived in Paris and representing the film company, offered Bergman the title role, that of a mysterious woman who may or may not be the real daughter of Czar Nicholas II, who, according to rumors, may have escaped the 1918 massacre of the Russian Imperial Family. Bergman wisely accepted this chance for a prestigious comeback to the Hollywood fold; and, on the other side of the coin, Hollywood was lucky to get her. During the summer of 1956, while she prepared her performance in the Anderson play, Bergman made *Anastasia* in Paris and London, under the direction of Russian-born Anatole Litvak.

Anastasia begins in Paris, in 1928. We are introduced to General Bounine (Brynner), a White Russian exile. With two confederates (Akim Tamiroff and Sacha Pitoeff), he hopes to find a likely young woman whom they can pass off as the missing Grand Duchess

CHAPTER IV

THE INTERNATIONAL YEARS

Anastasia and thereby collect for themselves some of the 10 million pound inheritance that the Czar is rumored to have deposited in banks outside Russia.

They find a promising candidate (Bergman) for their scheme in an impoverished, seemingly half-mad woman wandering about the St. Cloud section of Paris—a woman who remembers little of her past but who physically resembles what the Grand Duchess would look like, were she still living. The conspirators put their pupil under an intensive course of grooming and training in Romanov family habits and history. Strangely, the woman often anticipates minutiae of Romanov customs and individual traits. Bounine ascribes this to the woman's fevered imagination. Eventually, the time is ripe to present "Anastasia" to the Dowager Empress Marie (Helen Hayes), living in exile in Copenhagen with Prince Paul (Ivan Desny), her nephew, and the Baroness von Livenbaum (Martita Hunt), her lady-in-waiting. Inured to obvious imposters trying to pass themselves off as her granddaughter, the Dow-

ANASTASIA (1956). Between takes.

ANASTASIA (1956). With Akim Tamiroff, Yul Brynner, and Sacha Pitoeff.

ANASTASIA (1956). With Helen Hayes.

ANASTASIA (1956). With Yul Brynner.

ager Empress at first resists seeing the newest applicant for her official recognition.

Through the intercession of Prince Paul (who is not so much convinced of the claimant's authenticity as he is attracted to her) and the flighty but persuasive Baroness, the Dowager Empress at last agrees to grant an audience with the pretender. She almost dismisses her after hearing all the familiar bits of "inside" family gossip, when suddenly the young woman, in her anxiety, begins to cough. Recognizing this as a nervous habit of the real Anastasia, the old woman joyfully accepts her as her true granddaughter. Meanwhile, Anastasia—if that is who she really is—and Bounine, her promoter, have fallen in love and together they turn their back on the Romanov fortune and vanish from the scene forever. The Empress Dowager looks upon the elopement as final proof that the girl is Anastasia, for only royal blood would impetuously reject a fortune for love.

In mere summary, the story loses most of its impact. Bergman, after her transformation from a pathetic drab into the royal Anastasia, is breathtakingly beautiful —stately and dignified, but still a vulnerable woman who could easily renounce wealth and title for the man who rescued her from an aimless life. As the pitiable, haunted wanderer of the Paris streets, on the brink of drowning herself in the Seine (*Arch of Triumph* also began with Bergman about to do the same thing) she is completely convincing. As she picks up the information fed her by her coaches, her personality alters and becomes one of regal command and authority: "How dare you smoke in my presence!" she demands of a rattled Tamiroff, causing a skeptical former chamberlain of the Romanov court (Felix Aylmer) to ask with intrigued interest, "Who *are* you?"

Bergman's crucial confrontation with Hayes, the *raison d'être* of the play and film, is an almost operatic duet of insistent pleading, stern rejection, despair, and ultimate acceptance. It is acting in the grand manner and it is thrilling to watch. Up to the point where Bergman anticlimactically disappears (to account for historical fact), *Anastasia* is a gripping and altogether credible film.

Although Helen Hayes is undeniably a gifted actress, she is miscast as the Empress Dowager Marie. Her gestures are too small, her entire demeanor is too sweet-little-old-American-lady. In fact, there is someone in the cast who would have been splendid in the role. As the Baroness von Livenbaum, Martita Hunt is made fluttery and foolish ("It's madness without the moon," she gushes to Brynner at their daytime rendezvous in the Tivoli Gardens) but her gestures are grand and sweeping, she is magnificently self-aware, and she would have made an imposing Empress Dowager to match Bergman's Anastasia. Brynner is persuasive as the harshly demanding man who convinces the wanderer that she is, indeed, the lost Anastasia.

Alfred Newman's *Anastasia* theme is properly majestic and Slavic. Litvak's fast-paced direction succeeds in creating a world of half a century ago, one to which the viewer gladly gives up nearly two hours in willing suspension of disbelief. But it is Bergman's picture. Despair, suspicion, exhaustion, hysteria, self-doubt, self-confidence, and jubilation—the role calls for these emotions, and Bergman projects them all.

After *Anastasia* opened in December 1956, Bergman was welcomed back everywhere with overwhelming acclaim. Bosley Crowther, reviewing the picture in *The New York Times*, wrote that hers was "a beautifully molded performance, worthy of an Academy Award and particularly gratifying in the light of Miss Bergman's long absence from commendable films." Archer Winsten of the *New York Post* said, "*Anastasia* is a royal pud-

Arriving to accept New York Film Critics' Award.

ding of grand quality and Ingrid Bergman is the priceless plum in it." Alton Cook of the *New York World-Telegram* wrote, "Miss Bergman is the same torrent of passionate and impulsive ardor that she was before leaving American films."

Just before the film opened, the actress appeared before the Paris public in *Tea and Sympathy*. Audiences and critics praised her performance (and also her flawless French). The play ran from December 2, 1956, to July 10, 1957; then, after a month's summer holiday, through October.

On January 19, 1957—almost

Holding Award, with Kirk Douglas.

With Gary Cooper, Lars Schmidt, and Pia Lindstrom.

INDISCREET (1958). With Cary Grant, Cecil Parker, and Phyllis Calvert.

eight years after she had left the United States to meet Roberto Rossellini in Rome — Bergman arrived at New York's Idlewild Airport and was greeted by thousands of fans and theatrical colleagues. The occasion was the presentation to Bergman of the New York Film Critics' Award as the year's best actress, for her performance in *Anastasia*. And on March 27, the American Academy of Motion Picture Arts and Sciences presented her with a second Oscar. Cary Grant, who had loyally stood by Bergman during her "exile," received the award for her. (Bergman was back in Paris acting in *Tea and Sympathy*.) Grant said to the assembled Academy members, "It is a privilege to accept this award for so fine an actress. Dear Ingrid, if you can hear me via radio, all your friends here send you congratulations, love, admiration, and every affectionate thought."

Bergman was back at the top.

The following November, Bergman and Grant were reunited in a somewhat leaden soufflé called *Indiscreet*, a Warner Brothers adaptation of *Kind Sir*, Norman Krasna's romantic comedy starring Mary Martin and Charles Boyer that had entertained Broadway audiences. The movie displayed Bergman's still radiant beauty, neither she nor her costar looking as if

111

INDISCREET (1958). With Cary Grant.

INDISCREET (1958). As Ann Kalman.

Touring Italy with Pia Lindstrom.

more than a decade had passed since they appeared in *Notorious*. Produced and directed by Stanley Donen, best known for his direction of the musicals *On the Town, Singin' in the Rain,* and *Funny Face,* the movie deals with Ann Kalman (Bergman), a celebrated and wealthy actress, whose sister and brother-in-law (Phyllis Calvert and Cecil Parker) introduce her to Philip Adams (Cary Grant), an American banker-diplomat and eligible bachelor. Instantly attracted to one another, they embark on an affair, but to avoid marriage Philip tells Ann that he is already married. When she discovers that he is *not* married, she counters with a face-saving "fiancé" (David Kossoff), in reality her chauffeur. After several mixups and misunderstandings, Philip discovers the truth about Ann's "engagement," and proposes marriage.

Although the picture runs little more than an hour and a half, it seems much longer than that, despite the sprightly goings-on, the bright Technicolor world inhabited by the wealthy characters, and the cast's animated performances. "How *dare* he make love to me and not be a married man!" is the one outstanding line that Bergman is given to deliver. However, there is still pleasure in watching two professional actors at work. Since Bergman is clearly a talented *farceuse*, it is surprising that *Indiscreet* was her first Hollywood comedy. *The New York Times* remarked on the actress' talent for comedy: "Bergman emerges as a most charming comedienne, a professional who can handle a gaily irreverent line of dialogue as easily as a dramatic declamation."

Just before Bergman began *Indiscreet*, Kay Brown, her friend and confidante from the Selznick days, introduced the actress to a Swedish theatrical impresario named Lars Schmidt, who pro-

THE INN OF THE SIXTH HAPPINESS (1958). With director Mark Robson.

duced plays in Paris and Stockholm. Fellow Swedes with a shared passion for the theater, they quickly became friends. That summer of 1957, Pia, now nineteen, visited her mother. Together, they toured Italy, where in Taorima, Bergman received the Golden David of Donatello award for her performance in *Anastasia*.

Reunited after six years (Pia had spent a few days with her mother in London in 1951), they got along famously.

In March, 1958, Bergman began another picture for Twentieth Century-Fox, a lengthy, lavish, and successful version of the life of Gladys Aylward, a doughty British missionary to China in the early

THE INN OF THE SIXTH HAPPINESS (1958). With Curt Jurgens and Athene Seyler.

1930s. Cast as a former English chambermaid whose grit and unswerving dedication inspire her to lead a hundred Chinese orphans on a two-week cross-country trek, out of danger from Japanese invaders, Bergman was admirable. Her international costars were the British actor Robert Donat (he died of emphysema shortly after the film was completed) and Curt Jurgens, the German actor.

From Liverpool to London comes plain Gladys Aylward seeking a placement with the China Missionary Society. Rejected, she finds a job as a menial in the home of a retired explorer (Ronald Squire). By single-minded determination and radiant optimism, she persuades him to recommend her to an English missionary living in the mountains of North China. By scrimping, Gladys saves enough for the passage to China and finally arrives at the mission, a converted inn run by elderly Sara Lawson, (Athene Seyler). There, Gladys' enthusiasm for teaching the tenets of Christianity in a fairy-tale method earns her the name of Jan-Ai, The One Who Loves.

Meanwhile, Gladys has come to be a source of mild irritation to the local mandarin (Donat), who seeks to divert her proseletyzing by designating her as the official foot inspector, to enforce the new law forbidding the binding of female children's feet. She is so successful that the mandarin comes to respect and admire her. Gladys meets a Eurasian Chinese Army officer, Captain Lin Nan (Jurgens), who has come to the village to exhort the inhabitants to defend themselves against Japanese invaders. Despite his bitterness toward Westerners, he and Gladys are drawn to one another, and before leaving to rejoin the Chinese forces he gives her a jade ring as token of his love, promising that someday they will be reunited.

The Japanese attack and destroy the village by air and with troops. As an expression of his gratitude to Gladys for all that she has done for his people, the dying old mandarin

THE INN OF THE SIXTH HAPPINESS (1958). With Robert Donat.

becomes a Christian. Deeply moved, she says, "I thank you for this great gift." ("We shall not see each other again, I think," are Donat's last words as both the character he plays and, poignantly, as a film actor.) Gladys collects a small army of children and despite enemy air attacks and threats of danger on every hand, they arrive safely, amid cheers, at the mission, to face the man, now contrite, who first told her in London that she was unfit for missionary work. Gladys looks at the ring that Lin Nan gave her and with renewed

With Lars Schmidt and the Rossellini children, in December, 1959.

purpose starts the long trek back to the mission—The Inn of the Sixth Happiness, that place in the heart where everyone must decide his destiny.

There are many things wrong with the film, beginning with its excessive length. Every crisis (and there seems to be one at regular five-minute intervals) heralds the film's conclusion. Instead, under Mark Robson's indulgent direction, the picture so piles episode upon

episode that one's credulity is finally strained. At the outset, Bergman is depicted as the plainest of Janes, but as conditions worsen in China almost daily, she inexplicably becomes more and more breathtakingly beautiful. As crises and her unbroken string of accomplishments multiply—she quells a village jail riot, enlists the aid of a pack of cutthroat bandits against the Japanese, traverses mountains, and battles raging rivers while

118

assuming the responsibility of the orphans (remarkably well behaved and well scrubbed)—Gladys Aylward blooms and flourishes, assuming finally a transformation into Ingrid Bergman, the star of a CinemaScope and De Luxe Color epic. And yet, for all its flaws, *The Inn of the Sixth Happiness* is a moving and inspiring film. The mountainous landscape of Merionethshire, Wales, serves effectively as North China, adding greatly to the persuasiveness of the movie's physical production. John McCarten, writing in *The New Yorker*, summed up the picture best when he wrote: "Perhaps Miss Bergman,

all aglow with health and beauty, doesn't look like the sort of lady who might decide to devote her energies to missionary work, but as the film goes along, she radiates such honesty that we are willing to believe anything she wants us to."

After marrying Lars Schmidt in December 1958 (her marriage to Rossellini had been ruled void by an Italian court), Bergman divided her time between stage and television work and her family. In 1959, she made her American television debut as the enigmatic governess in James Costigan's excellent adaptation of *The Turn of the Screw*, a classic study in muted terror by

GOODBYE AGAIN (Aimez-vous Brahms?) (1961). With Jessie Royce Landis and Yves Montand.

GOODBYE AGAIN (Aimez-vous Brahms?) *(1961)*. With Françoise Sagan,
Anthony Perkins, director Anatole Litvak, and Yves Montand.

Henry James. For her performance, she was awarded the "Emmy" of the Academy of Television Arts and Sciences. In 1961, she appeared with Rip Torn in *Twenty-four Hours in a Woman's Life*, a badly received television version of a Stefan Zweig story.

Bergman's next film was 1961's *Goodbye Again*, based on *Aimez-vous Brahms?*, Françoise Sagan's attempt to equal the success of *Bonjour Tristesse*, her best-selling first novel.

Paula Tessier (Bergman), a middle-aged, prosperous Parisian interior decorator, has for several years been the faithful mistress of Roger Demarest (Yves Montand), who divides his time between Paula and other women. When Philip Van Der Besh (Anthony Perkins), a young American whose mother (Jessie Royce Landis) has engaged Paula's professional services, meets beautiful Paula, he is hopelessly smitten. Paula reciprocates his feelings and they begin an affair. When Demarest discovers their relationship, he offers to marry Paula. Realizing that she had been attracted to Philip for his youth and ardent expressions of love rather than out of any deep feeling, Paula marries Demarest. Devastated at the turn in events, Philip leaves Paula. Soon, she learns that marriage has not changed Demarest—again he makes excuses to leave her periodically for other women. Paula is now without love.

Goodbye Again is so thin and predictable (when, for example, Montand early in the picture smugly explains his unmarried relationship with Bergman—"because we both cherish our freedom too much"—there is danger ahead, spelled out in capital letters) that we are not lost for a moment in the action, but gaze instead at the dazzling Paris that director Anatole Litvak lets us see for the price of a movie ticket. We can admire only Bergman's Dior clothes and enjoy seeing again two fine supporting actresses, elegant Jessie Royce Landis and diamond-hard Lee Patrick.

Newspaper advertisements for *Goodbye Again* promised the cus-

With Trevor Howard in Hedda Gabler, *for television.*

With Rossellini twins, on set of THE VISIT.

tomer that he would see "Ingrid Bergman, Yves Montand, and Anthony Perkins shock the screen in a shameless affair!" But no one was shocked. And which one was the "shameless affair?" Bergman and Montand are well matched; their European accents help make believable to Americans European sexual mores. But as appealing as Perkins is as the infatuated youth (he was nearly thirty when the film was made), one cannot help wondering, irrelevantly, what a worldly woman like Ingrid Bergman could possibly see in the boyish Anthony Perkins. *The New York Times* expressed the incongruity of casting them together when it said, "[Bergman's] attitude all the way toward Mr. Perkins is that of a mother to a son."

The Paris critics were not favorable to Bergman's interpretation of the title role in Ibsen's *Hedda Gabler*, at the Théâtre Montparnasse, in 1962. Her portrayal of the destructive, neurotic wife of a dull scholar was seen on American television the following year. The distinguished cast included Sir Michael Redgrave, Sir Ralph Richardson, and Trevor Howard. Despite what many considered her brilliant projection of both malevolence and pathos, the actress received mixed notices from the television critics.

Bergman's next film venture was ill-advised. One of the dramatic successes of the 1958 Broadway season had been *The Visit*, a powerful play by the Swiss playwright and novelist Friedrich Duerrenmatt, in which Alfred Lunt and Lynn Fontanne gave brilliant performances. Set in contemporary Europe, it was a scathing indictment of the human capacity for greed and revenge. It tells what happens when a fabulously rich and well-known international courtesan returns to her native village, from which she was banished as a girl for allowing herself to be seduced. She enlists the villagers' aid, in return for an enormous sum of money to help the village's failing economy, in brutally executing the man who years before had betrayed her.

THE VISIT (1964). With Ernest Schroeder and Anthony Quinn.

THE VISIT (1964).
A publicity pose, as
Karla Zachanassian.

In 1964, Twentieth Century-Fox decided to film the play with Bergman in Rome's Cinecittà studios, in appropriately black-and-white Cinemascope. Bernhard Wicki, who had made *The Bridge,* a moving film about the drafting of small boys in the Nazis' last, desperate stages of defeat, was engaged as director. Although cast against type as Karla Zachanassian, *la belle dame sans merci,* Bergman's acting skill was sufficient to persuade the viewer that he sees before him not "wonderful Ingrid Bergman" but an amoral, heartless woman. However, the picture was an artistic—and commercial—disaster. Besides Wicki's uncertain direction, there was the crucial mistake of casting Anthony Quinn as Serge Miller, Karla's former lover. Quinn, a talented actor of long experience, is seen to best advantage in lusty, full-blooded roles such as Zorba the Greek. As a weak, bumbling shopkeeper who is sold out by his fellow villagers, Quinn is utterly unbelievable. In addition, Duerrenmatt's thematic statement that everyone—secular and ecclesiastical—has his price if it is high enough, was completely vitiated when Karla saves Serge from death at the last moment, feeling his guilt is punishment enough for the professional whoredom into which he unknowingly forced her.

Bergman was made up and cos-

THE VISIT (1964). As Karla Zachanassian.

THE YELLOW ROLLS-ROYCE (1965). With Omar Sharif.

tumed to look every inch "the richest woman in the world"— imperiously beautiful, magnificently gowned and jewelled, she alternately snapped and cooed her lines with much of Fontanne's commanding authority and icy charm. Where the play is a steadily mounting exercise in the cruelty that humankind can impose on its fellows, the movie is merely turgid and vaguely distasteful. Judith Crist was correct when, in reviewing *The Visit* for the *New York Herald Tribune*, she said that "the film has reduced this grisly horror story of greed and betrayal to the trivial, plotted terms of a woman's vengeance."

For her next film, Bergman joined with a dozen or so other stars (of greater and lesser brilliance) to appear in *The Yellow Rolls-Royce*, a three-part film in Panavision and Metrocolor that followed the fortunes of a handsome vintage automobile as it passed from owner to owner. The original screenplay was by the British playwright Terence Rattigan, whose

Separate Tables had been a great international success as play and movie. Anthony Asquith, who had directed the film versions of *The Winslow Boy* and *The Browning Version*, both Rattigan plays, was signed to guide the imposing cast through its paces.

A 1965 variation of *Tales of Manhattan*, Julien Duvivier's 1942 compendium movie about the wanderings of a tail coat, *The Yellow Rolls-Royce* is entertainment for those who like a two-hour feast consisting of adultery-among-the-rich, 1930s British-style (Episode I, with Rex Harrison, Jeanne Moreau, and Edmund Purdom), an American gangster and his cheating girl friend touring Italy (Episode II, with George C. Scott, Shirley MacLaine, Alain Delon, and Art Carney), and a wealthy, haughty American widow who learns humility and the excitement of a casual sexual encounter with a virtual stranger during the 1941 Nazi invasion of Yugoslavia (Episode III, with Bergman, Omar Sharif, and Joyce Grenfell). In each part, the sexual dénouement occurs in the back seat of the yellow-and-black car of the title.

Bergman's vignette is the best of the three. The actress, knowing she has only little more than half an hour to create a woman who undergoes near-instantaneous character reversal, delivers a min-

iature tour de force of acting. From being a fidgety, frigid anti-Roosevelt snob, whose sole interests seem to be doting on her pet Pekingese and patronizing her shy secretary-companion (Grenfell), Mrs. Gerda Millett becomes an ardent supporter of Yugoslavian guerrillas, using her car to transport them from one town to another. She also finds, into the bargain, a night of love in the car's back seat with a partisan fighter.

There were no surprises in the critical reception that the picture received. Most of the reviewers brushed aside the entire film as an anachronistic confection, out of touch with the world's grimmer realities. Nearly all of them, however, recognized the expertise of Bergman and Sharif in giving "this somewhat improbable adventure a lift by energetic and humorous delineations .... Miss Bergman's unrestrained dowager is forceful and impressive" (*The New York Times*).

Early in 1964, Bergman participated in another multi-story film that was a sentimental journey back to the Svenskfilmindustri studios, where she had begun her film career thirty years before. Called, rather sensationally, *Stimulantia*, it contained eight parts, one of them directed by Ingmar Bergman. The episode that Ingrid Bergman appeared in was "Smycket," an

STIMULANTIA ("Smycket," "The Necklace") (1967). With Gunnar Björnstrand.

In More Stately Mansions, *with Arthur Hill and Colleen Dewhurst.*

131

In The Human Voice, *for television.*

adaptation of "The Necklace," Guy de Maupassant's familiar short story. Her costar was Gunnar Björnstrand, a classmate from her School of the Royal Dramatic Theater days in the early thirties, and familiar to filmgoers for his starring appearances in many Ingmar Bergman pictures. In addition, the director of "Smycket" was Gustav Molander, who had directed Bergman in several films before she departed for Hollywood.

Released in 1967 (it has not yet been shown in the United States), *Stimulantia* occasioned a warm welcome by the Stockholm press of Bergman's return to the Swedish screen. Both *Chaplin* and *Expressen* remarked that "Ingrid Bergman is beautiful." with *Expressen* adding that "the crystal rings when she speaks." *Chaplin* praised the film as "a sober account in the best Svenskfilmindustri tradition."

In June 1965, Bergman helped to open the new Yvonne Arnaud Memorial Theatre in Guildford, England, in a production of Ivan Turgenev's *A Month in the Country*. Directed by Sir Michael Redgrave, it starred, in addition to Bergman and Redgrave, Max Adrian, Daniel Massey, and Fay Compton. In September, it moved to the Cambridge Theatre in London's West End, with Emlyn Williams and Jeremy Brett taking over for Adrian and Massey. Bergman

played Natalia Petrovna, the bored and restless woman in nineteenth-century Russia who flirts with a family friend and with her ward's handsome young tutor. Her attempts to infuse her life with romance and excitement prove futile and at the play's end she has no choice but to remain the discontented wife of a rich landowner. Of Bergman, the London *Times* said: "[She is] an actress impervious to changes of fashion and whose star quality as an ice goddess with warm human sympathies remains intact after a quarter of a century in the public eye. More than any other performer one can think of, she embodies a stable romantic ideal in the midst of change."

In 1930, Jean Cocteau wrote *La Voix Humaine (The Human Voice)*, an hour-long monodrama whose cast, action, and main prop consist only of an anguished woman talking, laughing, crying, pleading, and threatening, without respite, on the telephone in conversation with a lover who's leaving her. Bergman taped the play in London in 1966, and it was shown on American television in May 1967. She dedicated her performance to "the memory of my friend, Jean Cocteau," who died in 1963. *Variety* called Bergman's performance a "deeply felt study of a woman on the brink of suicide....The hour [was] memorable ... and records at

CACTUS FLOWER (1969). As Stephanie Dickinson.

CACTUS FLOWER (1969). With Goldie
Hawn and Walter Matthau.

CACTUS FLOWER (1969). With Walter Matthau.

the top of her form the warmth and skill of a considerable actress."

Bergman returned to the world of Eugene O'Neill in September 1967, when she appeared in Los Angeles and the following month in New York, at the Broadhurst Theatre, in *More Stately Mansions,* a previously unproduced work of the playwright. A far cry from the victimized Anna Christie whom she portrayed in 1941, her role in the later play cast her as a fiercely domineering matriarch of a rich and aristocratic New England family of the 1830s and 1840s. As the materialistic Deborah Harford, Bergman battled for control over her introverted and idealistic son Simon (Arthur Hill) against his equally determined wife Sara (Colleen Dewhurst). In the end, neither woman wins Simon over to her side and life goes on as before.

Clive Barnes of *The New York Times* expressed disappointment that Bergman's "very real inner goodliness (Miss Bergman has only to enter a stage—or, I am sure, a room—and any man with any blood or courtesy in him automatically starts to get up from his seat) ... makes less of the strangely disparate character of Deborah Harford than you might have hoped." On the other hand, Richard Watts, Jr., in the *New York Post,* praised her "skill and her characteristic charm."

After an absence of over twenty years, Bergman returned to Hollywood filmmaking in 1969 as the result of a two-picture contract with Columbia. The first movie was *Cactus Flower,* derived from the Broadway stage success by Abe Burrows who, in turn, had based his adaptation on a contemporary French farce by Barillet and Gredy. I. A. L. Diamond's screenplay retained most of the comic elements of Burrows' amusing script.

Stephanie Dickinson (Bergman) is secretary-nurse to Dr. Julian Winston (Walter Matthau), a prosperous New York dentist. Winston, a middle-aged man, imagines himself in love with Toni Simmons (Goldie Hawn), a kooky young Greenwich Village swinger. In order to sustain his affair with Toni and at the same time avoid marrying her, he asks Stephanie to pose as his wife and the mother of their children. Stephanie, who has been unavailingly in love with her boss for some years, welcomes the chance to be "Mrs. Winston," even if only temporarily. Deciding to look the part, and at the same time show Julian she is more than a dowdy office drudge, she transforms herself into a stunningly dressed woman, revealing her long-hidden beauty.

Then Julian, in order to staunch Toni's guilt that she is breaking up a happy home, enlists the help of

A WALK IN THE SPRING RAIN (1970). With Anthony Quinn and Tom Fielding.

his friend Harvey Greenfield (Jack Weston) to act as his "wife's" lover, hoping to prove to Toni that his marriage is in name only. Meanwhile, Toni has fallen in love with Igor Sullivan (Rick Lenz), a young writer who lives next door. One evening, at a discotheque, Julian and Toni encounter Stephanie with Harvey. "Mrs. Winston," looking radiant, enters into the spirit of the occasion by frugging with great exuberance with Igor, who has appeared on the scene, and then with Toni. At last, Julian awakens to Stephanie's dazzling radiance and congenial personality. Stephanie eventually tells Toni the truth and when Julian persists in desperately keeping up the masquerade, Toni tells him she knows all, but is in love with Igor. A wiser—and happier—man, Julian realizes he has come to love the woman he had for so long taken for granted.

Matthau's adeptness at wry comedy is nicely matched by Bergman's talents as a *farceuse*. Lauren Bacall, who had played Stephanie on the stage opposite Barry Nelson, brought an attractively sardonic, slightly "tougher" quality to the role. However, if Bergman's performance lacks anything, it is conviction as a mousy dental assistant in the film's early sequences. Her natural charm and beauty once given full reign, however, she adds a great deal to the enjoyment of *Cactus Flower*. Gene Saks' direction of the Technicolor film wisely let Bergman and Matthau be guided by their professional experience and considerable instinct for comedy. For her winsome, almost artless performance as Toni Simmons, Goldie Hawn won an Academy Award as the year's Best Supporting Actress.

In reviewing *Cactus Flower, The New York Times* commented that "the teaming of Matthau ... [with] the ultra-feminine Miss Bergman, in a rare comedy venture, was inspirational on somebody's part. ... The two stars mesh perfectly." The *New York Post* said of Bergman's performance, "As an efficient secretary, she's right on target, and when circumstances call for her to display the tribal-rock side of her personality, she gives it a good college try.... If she did more, it would be too much."

The other picture that Bergman made for Columbia, the following year, was *A Walk in the Spring Rain*. Its screenplay by Stirling Silliphant, based on a novel by Rachel Maddux, centers on a repressed professor's wife who finds unexpected love and tragedy in the hills of Tennessee.

Libby Meredith (Bergman) and her crotchety husband, Roger (Fritz Weaver), a Professor of Law, settle in the Smoky Mountains, where Roger plans to spend his

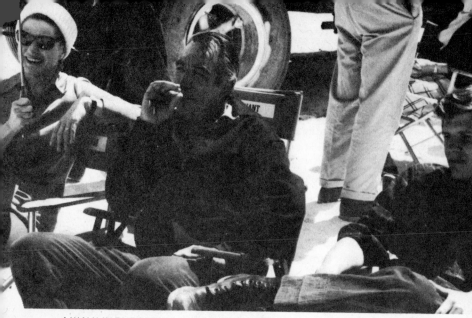

A WALK IN THE SPRING RAIN (1970). Between takes, with Anthony Quinn and Tom Fielding.

sabbatical writing a text book. There, they meet their neighbor and local handyman, Will Cade (Anthony Quinn), his wife, Annie (Virginia Gregg), and their son Boy (Tom Fielding), a young man in his twenties.

While Roger's writing takes up most of his time, Libby and Will gradually fall in love, and Libby's emotions are divided between her new-found happiness with a man who is passionate yet gentle, and guilt over her infidelity to her husband. Boy, who knows of the affair between his father and Libby, drunkenly confronts her and tries to make love to her. When Will

happens by and Boy threatens him with a gun, he accidentally kills his son. Later, sensing an estrangement between himself and his wife, Roger decides he and Libby will return to New York. Back home, Libby has only her memory of Will's parting words — "I'll just wait right here, 'cause I ain't going nowhere. And Libby, Libby, I ain't *never* going to die!" — and the love they shared.

Despite the triteness of its plot, there is much in *A Walk in the Spring Rain* to recommend it. Beyond Charles B. Lang's beautiful Technicolor photography of the Tennessee hills, there is the moving performance of Bergman as an intelligent and sensitive woman who, late in life, burgeons into sexual awakening. The viewer tends to forget the plot's predictability in watching the actress change from a patient, understanding wife and mother into a woman swept up in a passionate relationship. It is a role that any actress would find hard to make believable, but Bergman's skill makes Libby Meredith a credible and sympathetic character.

Quinn's performance as the unspoiled child of nature who kisses Sleeping Beauty awake (a comparison with Mellors in *Lady Chatterley's Lover* is inevitable) is one of his best. The two stars' romantic involvement in *A Walk in the Spring Rain* works far better than it did in *The Visit*.

The critics were generally unkind to the picture, expressing impatience with director Guy Green's lyric and leisurely pacing and regretting that it did not have the intensity of *Brief Encounter*, the film many of them contrasted with *A Walk in the Spring Rain*. In the *New York Post*, Archer Winsten observed that "Anthony Quinn and Ingrid Bergman are left out there wrestling with a script they can't quite make human and habitable." *The New York Times* called it "a dreary, tedious, unconvincing drama....Striving mightily and looking lovely, Miss Bergman seems merely a petulant woman who falls into the arms of Quinn for novelty, from boredom."

Bergman's most recent New York stage appearance was in April 1972, in a limited engagement of Bernard Shaw's *Captain Brassbound's Conversion*, at the Ethel Barrymore Theatre. She had already played the role of Lady Cicely Waynflete, a woman with a penchant for rearranging other people's lives to her own satisfaction, in London the previous year and, before coming to New York, at the Opera House of the Kennedy Center for the Performing Arts in Washington, D.C. All the critics praised Bergman, but most felt that Shaw's comedy of 1900 had dated badly. Of the New York production, Walter Kerr, writing in *The New York Sunday Times*, said that it was "a stock company production of an early Shaw play, put together on what seems less than a moment's notice to permit the ravishing Ingrid Bergman to place herself comfortably at center stage and glow." *Variety* noted that "the star is radiantly beautiful, but the Shaw comedy is antiquated.... She is not only visually stunning, however, but has a charming stage personality and gradually captivates the audience." *Time* magazine summed up concisely the star performance in a weak play: "Lovely to look at, graciously regal in bearing, exotically foreign in accent, [Bergman] does not remotely intend for any playwright to steal the spotlight."

"To survive in this business, you need a short memory and the constitution of an ox," Bergman once said. From being America's leading female star in 1946, and in the list of top ten actors and actresses in 1947 and 1948, she became box-office "poison" in the Rossellini years. With *Anastasia,* she made a triumphant comeback and a public with more sophisticated attitudes now found her to be fascinating for the very reasons it had condemned her ten years before.

More significant than such temporary ups and downs is the impressive fact that despite the undeniable weakness of some of Bergman's English-language films, half of them are, by the tabulation of *Variety's* 67th Anniversary Edition (1973), among the top money-making films of all time. The ten pictures, in descending order of film-rental earnings are: *Cactus Flower, The Bells of St. Mary's, For Whom the Bell Tolls, The Yellow Rolls-Royce, Anastasia, Spellbound, Notorious, The Inn of the Sixth Happiness, Saratoga Trunk,* and *Joan of Arc.* While it may seem surprising that *Casablanca* does not appear on the list, considering its enduring popularity and frequent showings today, it should be noted that studios often did not continue to report accumulated rentals after a film's initial release.

In recent years, Bergman has divided her career between films, the stage, television, and her family. Her children by her marriage to Rossellini live for the most part with their mother and stepfather at their country manor house in Choisel, France, twenty-five miles from Paris, and their house on Danholmen, off the coast of Sweden. At fifty-seven, Bergman became a grandmother when her daughter Pia, now Mrs. Joseph Daly and a newscaster for NBC television, gave birth to a son, Justin Christopher, on December 7, 1972.

Bergman has no desire to rest on her laurels. "I am not frightened by age," she says. "Just think of the wonderful parts I can play when I'm seventy." After more than forty years before the public, Bergman intends to go on working.

Ingrid Bergman once said she hoped that on her gravestone would appear the words: "She acted on the very last day of her life. Here rests a good actress." Bergman is far too modest; millions who have seen and admired her on the stage, on television, and above all on the screen, would insist that she is a great actress whose rare sensitivity and womanly warmth still cast their special glow.

A WALK IN THE SPRING RAIN (1970). As Libby Meredith.

143

BIBLIOGRAPHY

Agee, James. *Agee On Film*. Boston: Beacon Press, 1964.

"All-Time Boxoffice Champs." *Variety*, January 3, 1973.

Behlmer, Rudy, ed. *Memo from David O. Selznick*. New York: The Viking Press, 1972.

Bogdanovich, Peter. *The Cinema of Alfred Hitchcock*. New York: The Museum of Modern Art, 1963.

"'Captain Brassbound's Conversion.'" *Time*, May 1, 1972.

"'Captain Brassbound's Conversion.'" *Variety*, April 19, 1972.

Corliss, Richard, ed. *The Hollywood Screenwriters*. New York: Avon Books, 1972.

Davidson, Bill. *The Real and the Unreal*. New York: Harper & Brothers, 1961.

Guarner, José Luis. *Roberto Rossellini*. Translated by Elisabeth Cameron. New York: Praeger Publishers, Inc., 1970.

Higham, Charles, and Joel Greenberg. *The Celluloid Muse: Hollywood Directors Speak*. New York: New American Library, 1972.

Hollywood in the Forties. London: A. Zwemmer Limited, 1968.

Houseman, John. *Run-Through: A Memoir*. New York: Simon and Schuster, 1972.

Kerr, Walter. "Ravishing Bergman, Ravished Shaw." *The New York Sunday Times*, April 23, 1972.

Lambert, Gavin. *On Cukor*. New York: G. P. Putnam's Sons, 1972.

Leprohon, Pierre. *The Italian Cinema*. Translated by Roger Greaves and Oliver Stallybrass. New York: Praeger Publishers, Inc., 1972.

Jean Renoir. Translated by Brigid Elson. New York: Crown Publishers, Inc., 1971.

Macgowan, Kenneth. *Behind the Screen: The History and Techniques of the Motion Picture*. New York: Dell Publishing Co., Inc., 1965.

Maddux, Rachel, *et al. Fiction Into Film: "A Walk in the Spring Rain."* New York: Dell Publishing Co., Inc., 1972.

The New York Times Film Reviews: 1913-1968. Vols. 3, 4, 5. New York: The New York Times Company, 1970.

Perry, George. *The Films of Alfred Hitchcock*. London: Studio Vista Limited, 1965.

Quirk, Lawrence J. *The Films of Ingrid Bergman*. New York: The Citadel Press, 1970.

Ross, Lillian, and Helen Ross. *The Player: a Profile of an Art*. New York: Simon and Schuster, 1962.

Sarris, Andrew, ed. *Interviews with Film Directors*. New York: Avon Books, 1969.

Sennett, Ted. *Warner Brothers Presents*. New Rochelle: Arlington House. 1971.

Shipman, David. *The Great Movie Stars: The Golden Years*. New York: Crown Publishers, Inc., 1970.

Steele, Joseph Henry. *Ingrid Bergman: An Intimate Portrait*. New York: David McKay Company, Inc., 1959.

Taylor, John Russell. *Cinema Eye, Cinema Ear: Some Key Film-Makers of the Sixties*. New York: Hill and Wang, 1964.

Taylor, John Russell, ed. *Graham Greene on Film: Collected Film Criticism, 1935-1939*. New York: Simon and Schuster, 1972.

Thomas, Bob. *Selznick*. Garden City, New York: Doubleday & Company, Inc., 1970.

Truffaut, François. *Hitchcock*. New York: Simon and Schuster, 1966.

Vizzard, Jack. *See No Evil: Life Inside a Hollywood Censor*. New York: Simon and Schuster, 1970.

THE FILMS OF
INGRID BERGMAN

*The director's name follows the release date. A (c) following the release date indicates
that the film was in color. Sp indicates Screenplay and b/o indicates based/on.*

1. MUNKBROGREVEN(*The Count of the Monk's Bridge*),Svenskfilmindustri, 1934, *Edvin Adolphson and Sigurd Vallen*. Sp: Gosta Stevens, b/o play *Greven fran Gamla Sta'n* by Arthur and Sigfried Fischer. Cast: Valdemar Dahlquist, Sigurd Wallen, Edvin Adolphson. Bergman in a minor role as a hotel maid.

2. BRANNINGAR (*The Surf*),Svenskfilmindustri, 1935, *Ivar Johansson*. Sp: Ivar Johansson, b/o idea by Henning Ohlssen. Cast: Sten Lindgren, Tore Svennberg, Carl Strom. Fisherman's daughter (Bergman) raises her and minister's illegitimate child.

3. SWEDENHIELMS (*The Swedenhielm Family*), Svenskfilmindustri, 1935, *Gustav Molander*. Sp: Stina Bergman, b/o play by Hjalmar Bergman. Cast: Gosta Ekman, Karin Swanstrom, Bjorn Berglund, Hakan Westergren. Wealthy girl (Bergman) wins love of poor but proud scientist's son.

4. VALBORGSMASSOAFTON (*Walpurgis Night*), Svenskfilmindustri, 1935, *Gustav Edgren*. Sp: Oscar Rydquist and Gustaf Edgren, b/o their original story. Cast: Lars Hanson, Victor Seastrom, Karin Carlsson. Bergman in love with unhappily married man.

5. PA SOLSIDAN (*On the Sunny Side*), Svenskfilmindustri, 1936, *Gustav Molander*. Sp: Oscar Hemberg and Gosta Stevens, b/o play by Helge Krog. Cast: Lars Hanson, Edvin Adolphson, Marianne Lofgren. Bergman as woman who inadvertently causes husband pangs of jealousy.

6. INTERMEZZO, Svenskfilmindustri, 1936, *Gustav Molander*. Sp: Gustav Molander and Gosta Stevens, b/o story by Gustav Molander. Cast: Gosta Ekman, Inga Tidblad, Hugo Bjorne. Bergman as concert pianist who has love affair with married violinist.

7. DOLLAR, Svenskfilmindustri, 1938, *Gustav Molander*. Sp: Stina Bergman and Gustav Molander, b/o play by Hjalmar Bergman. Cast: Georg Rydeberg, Kotti Chave, Tutta Rolf, Hakan Westergren. Bergman as wife of wealthy businessman, both involved in marital mixups.

8. EN KVINNAS ANSIKTE *(A Woman's Face)*, Svenskfilmindustri, 1938, *Gustav Molander*. Sp: Gosta Stevens, b/o play *Il Etait Une Fois* by François de Croisset. Cast: Anders Henrikson, Gunnar Sjoberg,, Georg Rydeberg. Facially scarred blackmailer (Bergman) is restored to beauty and respectability. Remade by MGM in 1941, with Joan Crawford.

9. DIE VIER GESELLEN *(The Four Companions)*, UFA, 1938, *Carl Froelich*. Sp: Jochun Huth, b/o play by Jochun Huth. Cast: Carsta Lock, Sabine Peters, Ursula Herking, Hans Sohnker, Leo Slezak. Career woman (Bergman) gives up advertising for marriage.

10. EN ENDA NATT *(Only One Night)*, Svenskfilmindustri, 1939, *Gustav Molander*. Sp: Gosta Stevens, b/o story *En Eneste Natt* by Harald Tandrup. Cast: Edvin Adolphson, Olof Sandborg, Aino Taube. Ward (Bergman) of wealthy aristocrat resists advances of his illegitimate son.

11. INTERMEZZO: A LOVE STORY, Selznick International-United Artists, 1939, *Gregory Ratoff*. Sp: George O'Neil, b/o Sp by Gosta Stevens and Gustav Molander. Cast: Leslie Howard, Edna Best, John Halliday, Cecil Kellaway. Selznick's remake of the Swedish film and Bergman's American screen debut.

12. JUNINATTEN *(A June Night)*, Svenskfilmindustri, 1940, *Per Lindberg*. Sp: Ragnar Hylten-Cavallius, b/o story by Tora Nordstrom-Bonnier. Cast: Gunnar Sjoberg, Carl Strom, Olof Widgren. After suffering near-death at hands of brutish lover, girl (Bergman) finds happiness with understanding man.

13. ADAM HAD FOUR SONS, Columbia, 1941, *Gregory Ratoff*. Sp: William Hurlbut and Michael Blankfort, b/o novel *Legacy* by Charles Bonner. Cast: Warner Baxter, Fay Wray, Susan Hayward, Helen Westley, Richard Denning. French governess (Bergman) earns family's devotion and love of its widowed father.

14. RAGE IN HEAVEN, MGM, 1941, *W. S. Van Dyke II*. Sp: Christopher Isherwood and Robert Thoeren, b/o novel by James Hilton. Cast: Robert Montgomery, George Sanders, Lucile Watson, Oscar Homolka. Bergman as wife of psychotic husband who suspects her of infidelity.

15. DR. JEKYLL AND MR. HYDE, MGM, 1941, *Victor Fleming*. Sp: John Lee Mahin, b/o novel by Robert Louis Stevenson. Cast: Spencer Tracy, Lana Turner, Donald Crisp, Ian Hunter. Bergman as barmaid victim of evil Mr. Hyde.

16. CASABLANCA, Warners, 1942, *Michael Curtiz*. Sp: Julius J. and Philip G. Epstein and Howard Koch, b/o play *Everybody Comes to Rick's* by Murray Burnett and Joan Alison. Cast: Humphrey Bogart, Paul Henreid, Claude Rains, Peter Lorre, Sydney Greenstreet. Bergman as woman torn between love for café owner and duty to husband.

17. SWEDES IN AMERICA, Office of War Information, 1943, *Irving Lerner*. Documentary made for OWI's Overseas Motion Picture Bureau. Bergman visits Swedish farming families in Minnesota.

18. FOR WHOM THE BELL TOLLS, Paramount, 1943, (c), *Sam Wood*. Sp: Dudley Nichols, b/o novel by Ernest Hemingway. Cast: Gary Cooper, Katina Paxinou, Akim Tamiroff, Vladimir Sokoloff. Bergman as heroine Maria caught up in romance and intrigue during Spanish Civil War.

19. GASLIGHT, MGM, 1944, *George Cukor*. Sp: John Van Druten, Walter Reisch, John L. Balderston, b/o play *Angel Street* by Patrick Hamilton. Cast: Charles Boyer, Joseph Cotten, Angela Lansbury, Dame May Whitty. Bergman as tormented wife of murderous thief.

20. THE BELLS OF ST. MARY'S, RKO, 1945, *Leo McCarey*. Sp: Dudley Nichols, b/o story by Leo McCarey. Cast: Bing Crosby, Henry Travers, Ruth Donnelly, William Gargan. Bergman as nun who learns deeper human understanding from priest.

21. SPELLBOUND, Selznick-United Artists, 1945, *Alfred Hitchcock*. Sp: Ben Hecht, adapted by Angus MacPhail, b/o novel *The House of Dr. Edwardes* by Francis Beeding. Cast: Gregory Peck, Leo G. Carroll, Michael Chekhov. Psychiatrist (Bergman) helps lead guilt-ridden amnesiac back to sanity.

22. SARATOGA TRUNK, Warners, 1945, *Sam Wood*. Sp: Casey Robinson, b/o novel by Edna Ferber. Cast: Gary Cooper, Flora Robson, Jerry Austin, Florence Bates, John Warburton. Creole adventuress (Bergman) finds romance at Saratoga Springs.

23. NOTORIOUS, RKO, 1946, *Alfred Hitchcock*. Sp: Ben Hecht. Cast: Cary Grant, Claude Rains, Madame Konstantin. German spy's daughter (Bergman) joins dangerous mission to expose Nazi refugees in Rio de Janeiro.

24. ARCH OF TRIUMPH, Enterprise-United Artists, 1948, *Lewis Milestone*. Sp: Lewis Milestone and Harry Brown, b/o novel by Erich Maria Remarque. Cast: Charles Boyer, Charles Laughton, Louis Calhern, Stephen Bekassy. Demimondaine (Bergman), saved from suicide by man who loves her, reverts to immorality.

25. JOAN OF ARC, Sierra Pictures-RKO, 1948, (c), *Victor Fleming*. Sp:

Maxwell Anderson and Andrew Solt, adapted from play *Joan of Lorraine* by Maxwell Anderson. Cast: José Ferrer, Francis L. Sullivan, Shepperd Strudwick, Cecil Kellaway. Bergman as French heroine burned at the stake.

26. UNDER CAPRICORN, Transatlantic-Warners, 1949, (c), *Alfred Hitchcock*. Sp: James Bridie, adapted by Hume Cronyn, b/o novel by Helen Simpson. Cast: Joseph Cotten, Michael Wilding, Margaret Leighton, Cecil Parker. Weak-willed woman (Bergman) trapped in unhappy marriage.

27. STROMBOLI, RKO, 1950, *Roberto Rossellini*. Sp: Roberto Rossellini, with Art Cohn, Renzo Cesana, Mario Sponza. Bergman as fisherman's wife who rebels against primitive life on an Italian island.

28. EUROPA '51 *(The Greatest Love)*, Ponti-De Laurentiis, 1951, I. F. E. Releasing Corp., 1954 (U.S.), *Roberto Rossellini*. Sp: Roberto Rossellini, Sandro de Leo, Mario Pannunzio, Ivo Perilli, Brunello Rondi. Cast: Alexander Knox, Ettore Giannini, Giulietta Masina. After son's death, philanthropy-obsessed woman (Bergman) is considered insane.

29. SIAMO DONNE *(We, the Women)*, Titanus, 1953, *Roberto Rossellini*. Sp: Cesare Zavattini and Luigi Chiarini (Bergman segment). Cast: Albamarie Setaccioli. In third ("Ingrid Bergman") of five-episode film, Bergman protects her rose garden from ravenous hen.

30. VIAGGIO IN ITALIA *(Journey to Italy)*, Titanus, 1954, shown in U.S. as *Strangers*, 1955, *Roberto Rossellini*. Sp: Roberto Rossellini and Vitaliano Brancati. Cast: George Sanders, Paul Muller, Anna Proclemer. After attending religious festival in Naples, English woman (Bergman) and husband decide not to part.

31. GIOVANNA D'ARCO AL ROGO *(Joan of Arc at the Stake)*, Produzione Cinematografiche Associate (Rome), Franco-London Film (Paris), 1954, (c), *Roberto Rossellini*, b/o oratorio by Arthur Honegger and Paul Claudel. Cast: Tullio Carminati, Giacinto Prandelli, Saturno Meletti. Bergman in speaking part as the martyred Joan.

32. ANGST *(Fear)*, Minerva, 1955, *Roberto Rossellini*. Sp: Roberto Rossellini, Sergio Amidei, Franz Graf Treuberg, b/o story by Stefan Zweig. Cast: Mathias Wiedmann, Renate Mannhardt, Kurt Kreuger. Bergman as woman involved in adultery and blackmail.

33. ELENA ET LES HOMMES *(Elena and Men)*, Franco-London Film/Films Gibé (Paris) Electra Compania Cinematografica (Rome), 1956, (c), released as *Paris Does Strange Things* in U.S., Warners, 1957, *Jean Renoir*. Sp: Jean Renoir. Cast: Jean Marais, Mel Ferrer, Juliette Greco. Bergman as a Polish princess in Paris who dabbles in political intrigue.

34. ANASTASIA, 20th Century-Fox, 1956, (c), *Anatole Litvak*. Sp: Arthur Laurents, b/o play by Marcelle Maurette adapted by Guy Bolton. Cast: Yul Brynner, Helen Hayes, Martita Hunt, Akim Tamiroff. Bergman as drifter in Paris passed off as heir to the Romanov fortune.

35. INDISCREET, Warners, 1958, (c), *Stanley Donen*. Sp: Norman Krasna, b/o play *Kind Sir* by Norman Krasna. Cast: Cary Grant, Cecil Parker, Phyllis Calvert, David Kossoff. Romantic misunderstandings between famous actress (Bergman) and American diplomat.

36. THE INN OF THE SIXTH HAPPINESS, 20th Century-Fox, 1958, (c), *Mark Robson*. Sp: Isobel Lennart, b/o novel *The Small Woman* by Alan Burgess. Cast: Robert Donat, Curt Jurgens, Athene Seyler, Ronald Squire. Missionary (Bergman) in China leads orphans to safety during Japanese invasion.

37. GOODBYE AGAIN, United Artists, 1961, *Anatole Litvak*. Sp: Samuel Taylor, b/o novel *Aimez-vous Brahms?* by Françoise Sagan. Cast: Yves Montand, Anthony Perkins, Jessie Royce Landis. Fashionable interior decorator (Bergman) leaves lover for affair with young American.

38. THE VISIT, 20th Century-Fox, 1964, *Bernhard Wicki*. Sp: Ben Barzman, b/o play by Friedrich Duerrenmatt. Cast: Anthony Quinn, Irina Demick, Valentina Cortese, Ernest Schroeder. Fabulously rich woman (Bergman) bribes poor village to kill man who betrayed her.

39. THE YELLOW ROLLS-ROYCE, MGM, 1965, (c), *Anthony Asquith*. Sp: Terence Rattigan. Cast: Omar Sharif, Joyce Grenfell, Wally Cox. In final episode of three-part film, wealthy American widow (Bergman) has fleeting war-time affair with anti-Nazi Yugoslavian partisan fighter.

40. STIMULANTIA ("Smycket") Omnia, 1967, *Gustav Molander*. Sp: Gustav Molander, b/o "The Necklace" by Guy de Maupassant. Cast: Gunnar Björnstrand, Gunnel Brostrom. In eight-part film, poor woman (Bergman) and husband save for years to replace lost diamond necklace, only to find that it was a paste imitation.

41. CACTUS FLOWER, Columbia, 1969 (c), *Gene Saks*. Sp: I. A. L. Diamond, b/o play by Abe Burrows, adapted from play by Barillet and Gredy. Cast: Walter Matthau, Goldie Hawn, Jack Weston, Rick Lenz. Plain dental assistant (Bergman) blooms into beauty and marries her boss.

42. A WALK IN THE SPRING RAIN, Columbia, 1970, (c), *Guy Green*. Sp: Stirling Silliphant, b/o novel by Rachel Maddux. Cast: Anthony Quinn, Fritz Weaver, Katherine Crawford, Tom Fielding, Virginia Gregg. Law professor's wife (Bergman) finds brief happiness in affair with handyman in Tennessee hills.

INDEX

(Page numbers italicized indicate photographs)

152

153

155

157

ABOUT THE AUTHOR

Curtis F. Brown has been a film addict for many years and an Ingrid Bergman fan since his teens. Administrative assistant at a New York college, he lives in a restored 1840's house in Brooklyn.

ABOUT THE EDITOR

Ted Sennett has been attending and enjoying movies since the age of two. He has written about films for magazines and newspapers, and is the author of *Warner Brothers Presents*, a survey of the great Warners films of the thirties and forties. A publishing executive, he lives in New Jersey with his wife and three children.